The Hillbilly Kitchen Verses and Vittles

By: Becky Walker

There is a video for every recipe on

The Hillbilly Kitchen

Down Home Country Cooking

And Jesus said unto them, I am the bread of life: he that cometh to me shall never hunger; and he that believeth on me shall never thirst. – John 6:35

Book cover written and created by Bret Walker

The Lord's Prayer

[9] After this manner therefore pray ye: Our Father which art in heaven, Hallowed be thy name.

[10] Thy kingdom come, Thy will be done in earth, as it is in heaven.

[11] Give us this day our daily bread.

[12] And forgive us our debts, as we forgive our debtors.

[13] And lead us not into temptation, but deliver us from evil: For thine is the kingdom, and the power, and the glory, forever. Amen.

Matthew 6

A good way to start the day or a book

Dedication

The story of The Hillbilly Kitchen is an example of how God works all things for the good of those who love Him. Every event in my life has been to prepare me for what I am doing today. All of the trials, triumphs, mistakes (mine not Gods) and experiences have led me to this unseen, unimagined destiny.

My childhood by today's standards would be considered less than ideal but had things been perfect I would have been a far different person. Most people would consider getting married at 17 to a 23 year old divorced man and having four children in five years a life ending mistake, not a life altering decision. This choice is what led me to my knees at 24 years of age.

At 24 I was expecting my fourth baby and my oldest was only four. I was in a truly hopeless situation. I don't want to go into all of the details, but death seemed preferable to my life at the time. The 700 Club was on the television one day and I overheard them talking about how God could fix any problem. I don't remember exactly what was said, but they were offering hope. I prayed with them and then I had a personal conversation with God. Again, I don't remember everything exactly, but there was hope from that moment, and that was the beginning of my relationship with God and His Son Jesus.

I know in my heart that there was not another man in the entire world who could have traveled this journey with me and helped me reach this point in my life. While the early years of our marriage were difficult to say the least, Bret saw things in me that I did not know existed and he believed I could be more than I could imagine. Throughout the course of our life together, he always encouraged me to do things that were far beyond what I thought I was capable of. I had many hobbies and jobs that involved teaching which seems to be my natural gift. However, I have always been a very shy person, yet Bret somehow saw a public speaker.

One of only two portraits that Bret and I have ever had taken together.

During the time while we operated our karate school, he always had me do announcements and promotion ceremonies. After a few years, we began to take a small group of children to schools to do demonstrations. He was always conveniently busy so I would have to speak before gymnasiums filled with people during these demonstrations. This led to a ministry that involved our entire family and even more public speaking, this time it involved public speaking under a spotlight for God. Our ministry was named "Team Trinity Martial Arts Ministry".

Promotion night when my 3 youngest daughters all earned their Black Belts

After our kids grew up and left home, my life seemed empty, mostly because it seemed my work for God had ended. My children were raised and had outgrown the ministry we were all involved in. I really had no idea what the rest of my life was going to hold. I had always thought that once my children were grown I would have time for a career. I even went back to college in my forties after which I discovered there aren't many entry level positions for middle aged people.

Even though I had no idea which way to turn, Bret saw my future and my purpose. For years he pushed me to make cooking videos for YouTube. After years of relentless encouragement (nagging), one snowy, February day, I relented and made a snow cream video. I thought that would end this silly nonsense. To my amazement people watched it and Bret continued his encouragement. So I continued the videos.

After several months we realized that not only were people watching but they were listening to what I was saying. It was at this point that I knew God had given me a great ministry opportunity. Over the years the video quality and substance has evolved and improved, this progression has been mostly due to Bret's vision. That day, 34 years ago when I met him, God knew that Bret was the only man in the world who could walk with me and help to form me into the person who I needed to be in order to fill His ministry.

While Bret's persuasive powers are considerable, those of you who watch the YouTube videos and take the time to leave kind, encouraging, supportive and inspirational comments are the reason that the videos have continued and will continue for as long as possible. THANK YOU!

I want to especially thank those of you who came by YesterYear Country Market during the two years while I worked there. It was your visits and your personal contact that truly convinced me that this was what I should be doing with my life and it was a true calling from God. It was the impact of these visits which lead to this actually becoming a career.

I also want to thank my girls. For some reason they have always believed I was better than I really am and could do almost anything. Their faith in me has always been an encouragement and pushed me to try a little harder and do a little more. I want them to know that they will always be my greatest achievement and my greatest source of pride. I love you all!

My amazing beautiful daughters

When I look back over the past, even before my life began, I can see God's hand working to lead me to where I am today and I know without any doubt that He is in control of all that has been, is, or will be. I thank God every day for my salvation and His purpose and direction in my life. **Jesus is my Lord!**

Many of you will wonder why I didn't talk about my mom. I will be going into detail about my mother and our relationship in the next book. I learned the value of my mother way too late and I believe many people will benefit from hearing our story and struggles.

Special thanks to my mother-in-law, Ann Walker for giving me my husband, and for helping me type this book

[3] Honour widows that are widows indeed. [4] But if any widow have children or nephews, let them learn first to shew piety at home, and to requite their parents: for that is good and acceptable before God. [5] Now she that is a widow indeed, and desolate, trusteth in God, and continueth in supplications and prayers night and day. - 1Timothy5

Contents:

There hath no temptation taken you but such as is common to man: but God *is* faithful, who will not suffer you to be tempted above that ye are able; but will with the temptation also make a way to escape, that ye may be able to bear *it*.

1 Corinthians 10:13

Perfect Pot Roast

Ingredients: 2 pound beef roast · 1 ½ pounds carrots · 2 pounds potatoes · large onion · salt · pepper · garlic powder · Worcestershire sauce · 2 or 3 tablespoons corn starch

This recipe will work with any beef roast. You can use any carrots and potatoes, but baby carrots and new potatoes taste better and cut down on preparation time and effort. I usually prepare 8 ounces of beef per person, and 6 ounces of carrots and 6 ounces of potatoes per person (per-cooked weight). I always use yellow onions and you can add more or less to taste. You will also need salt, pepper, garlic powder or fresh garlic, Worcestershire sauce and cornstarch. I cook the roast, along with the onions, garlic or garlic powder, Worcestershire sauce, salt and pepper slowly and for a long time which makes it very tender, at least an hour per pound. Keep a lid on your roast while it is cooking. It should have plenty of moisture in it but, if your pot starts to get dry you may need to add water from time to time to keep it from burning. Once the roast is tender add the carrots and add a little water if needed. Let the carrots cook about ½ done add the potatoes and enough water to almost cover all the veggies. Combine the corn starch and about ½ cup of cold water. Once the veggies are done slowly add the corn starch mixture to the pot. If you are making a smaller or larger roast adjust the corn starch. A little corn starch will thicken a lot of liquid. So when you are making your gravy add your corn starch mixture slowly and stop as soon as it starts to thicken. Over time you will learn exactly how much you need. If you get it too thick you can add a little water to thin it, but don't get carried away or it will lose flavor. Also if you need to prepare part of it ahead of time you can cook the roast to the point where it is ready to add the veggies the day before your dinner, but if you do this put the whole pot in the fridge because you will want ALL the brown stuff in the pan to flavor the veggies.

This has been a Christmas tradition in our home for 30 years. It is very easy to make and doesn't require constant attention, so I don't have to spend all day in the kitchen. It is easy to keep warm so it is ready to eat and hot as guests arrive and the leftover roast makes great sandwiches. We started having it for Christmas because my kids wanted roast "beast" like the Grinch had, and they still call it Christmas Roast Beast to this day.

Oven Roasted Turkey

Ingredients: Turkey Ingredients: Turkey · ¼ cup Honey · ¼ cup Lemon juice · 2 tablespoons Onion powder · Salt & pepper

Remove neck and giblets from turkey and wash the turkey well. Combine all other ingredients in a jar with a lid and shake until well combined. Put turkey in pan and pour half
of seasonings inside turkey and cover outside of turkey with the remaining half. Cover turkey tightly with heavy duty foil and place in a pre-heated 350° oven for 20-25 minutes
per pound. Once turkey is done and tender you can remove the foil and brown the turkey under the broiler but it is not necessary. Once you have removed the turkey from the oven, dip the broth out of the pan and pour it over the turkey several times. This will make the turkey moist.

Gravy Ingredients: 3 cups Broth from the turkey pan · ½ cup Cold water · 2 or 3 tablespoons Corn starch · Onion powder Salt & pepper

Put the broth in a pot over medium heat. Combine corn starch and cold water, stir until well combined. Slowly add corn starch mixture to broth while stirring pot. Continue to stir until pot boils and gravy thickens. Add salt, pepper and onion powder to taste.

Tip: make sure turkey is completely thawed. If it is still partially frozen it will be tough and chewy.

Tip: make sure to wash hands and all surfaces in the kitchen that the raw turkey might have touched or dripped on. Raw poultry can cause serious illness.

In every thing give thanks: for this is the will of God in Christ Jesus concerning you. - 1 Thessalonians 5:18

Country Fried Steak

Ingredients:

1 1/4 pound - Ground round (Lean)
1/2 to 1 cup - Flour (Any kind)
1/4 to 1/3 cup - Ground flax seed
2 cups - Milk
Salt
Pepper
Onion powder
1 to 2 tablespoons of oil

Therefore I say unto you, Take no thought for your life, what ye shall eat, or what ye shall drink; nor yet for your body, what ye shall put on. Is not the life more than meat, and the body than raiment?
Matthew 6:25

- Divide beef into 4 to 6 equal portions and shape into thin oblong patties
- Mix ¼ cup flour and ¼ cup of flax seed
- Season both sides of beef with salt, pepper and onion powder and roll in flour mixture
- While meat is resting, lightly coat skillet with oil and pre-heat on medium heat
- Once skillet is pre-heated place meat in skillet and brown well on both sides
- Remove meat from skillet and place on rack to drain
- Add ¼ cup of flour, salt, pepper and onion powder to skillet
- Stir until grease in skillet has been absorbed into flour
- Pour milk into skillet all at once and stir until flour mixture is will combined with milk – a whisk works well for this process
- Continue stirring until mixture comes to a boil and reaches desired consistency
- If mixture is too thick more milk can be added, if it is too thin continue to boil and it will thicken – keep in mind that gravy thickens as it cools
- Place meat on a plate and cover in gravy

Every good gift and every perfect gift is from above, and cometh down from the Father of lights, with whom is no variableness, neither shadow of turning. - James 1:17

Stuffed Peppers

Ingredients:

6 Green bell peppers
2 lbs. Ground beef (any grade) · 1 Good size chopped onion
3 Cups of water · 1 1/2 Cups Long grain rice
2 Tablespoons of real butter · 17 ounces Tomato soup
2 to 3 cups Shredded cheddar cheese
Salt & pepper

That He would grant you, according to the riches of His glory, to be strengthened with might by His Spirit in the inner man; That Christ may dwell in your hearts by faith; that ye, being rooted and grounded in love.
Ephesians 3:16-17

- Combine beef, onion, salt and pepper in skillet and cook until beef is brown and crumbled, then drain grease
- Bring water, butter and salt to a boil in separate pot, add rice, cover and cook for 20 minutes on low heat without uncovering
- Cut peppers in half, wash and clean seeds out
- Put peppers in large pot, cover with water and bring to a boil for 3 or 4 minutes
- Combine drained beef, cooked rice, tomato soup and 2 cups of cheese
- Drain water from peppers and place peppers in large lightly oiled or sprayed casserole pan or baking pan
- Fill each pepper half with the beef and rice mixture and mound up on top
- Any extra mixture can be placed in pan in the gaps around the stuffed peppers
- Top the stuffed peppers with the remaining cup of cheese
- Bake in a preheated 350° oven for 45 to 60 minutes until golden brown

The Lord shall preserve thee from all evil:
He shall preserve thy soul.
The Lord shall preserve thy going out and thy coming in
from this time forth, and even for evermore.
Psalm 121:7-8

Sloppy Joes

Ingredients:

2 lb. - Ground beef or ground chuck
1/2 cup - Ketchup
1/2 cup - BBQ sauce
Onion powder
Salt and pepper

- In a skillet combine beef, salt, pepper and onion powder
- Cook over medium heat until beef is brown and well done
- Drain grease
- Return skillet to stove and add ketchup and BBQ sauce
- Stir and continue to cook until mixture is thoroughly heated

21 Then came Peter to him, and said, Lord, how oft shall my brother sin against me, and I forgive him? till seven times?

22 Jesus saith unto him, I say not unto thee, Until seven times: but, Until seventy times seven. - Matthew 18

Skillet Steak

Ingredients:

Steak
Salt & pepper
Onion powder

A sliced onion may be added on top of steak at the beginning of cooking for additional flavor

- Tenderize steak with a meat tenderizer by pounding both sides
- Season both sides of steak
- Place steaks in a lightly oiled or sprayed pre-heated skillet on medium heat
- Cover and cook without turning until meat is tender and browned on first side
- Turn meat over and cook until second side is brown
- Cut a small slit in center of steak to make sure it is cooked to safe and desired degree

And above all things have fervent charity among yourselves: for charity shall cover the multitude of sins. - 1 Peter 4:8

S.O.S.

Ingredients:

Toast
1 lb. Ground beef
1/4 Cup Flour
2 Cups Milk
Onion Powder
Salt and Pepper

- In a skillet combine ground beef, onion powder, salt and pepper
- Cook until beef is brown and well done
- Remove excess grease
- Add flour, additional salt and pepper to beef stir until well combined
- Add milk all at once and stirring constantly on medium heat, cook until boiling and thick
- Serve over toast

"And I looked, and rose up, and said unto the nobles, and to the rulers, and to the rest of the people, Be not ye afraid of them: remember the Lord, *which is* great and terrible, and fight for your brethren, your sons, and your daughters, your wives, and your houses." - Nehemiah 4:14

Meatloaf

Ingredients:
2 lbs. Ground beef
1/4 Cup ketchup
1 Cup BBQ sauce
1 Sleeve Saltine crackers
2 Eggs
1 Green bell pepper
1 Onion
1/2 Cup ground flax seed
Salt, pepper and onion powder to taste

- In a large bowl beat eggs slightly
- Crush crackers, chop pepper and onion
- Add all ingredients to bowl, except ½ cup of BBQ sauce and mix well
- Press ingredients into oven safe skillet or oven safe baking dish
- Cover and bake in 350° oven for 1 hour
- Uncover top with remaining BBQ sauce, and continue to bake 1 hour

Giving thanks always for all things unto God and the Father in the name of our Lord Jesus Christ - Ephesians 5:20

Chili

Ingredients:

1 1/2 lbs ground
beef
1 onion chopped
2 bell peppers
chopped
1 can kidney
beans
2 cans pinto beans
1 can tomato of
your choice (can
or fresh)
chili powder
salt, pepper &
sugar to taste

- Combine beef, peppers, onions, salt and pepper in a large pot and cook until beef is done and crumbled - drain excess grease
- Add beans, tomatoes and spices to pot
- Bring to a boil, reduce heat, cover and simmer for 30 minutes to several hours
- Stir occasionally and taste to adjust spices
- Add a little water if it starts to get to thick while simmering

Be kindly affectioned one to another with brotherly love; in honour preferring one another. - Romans 12:10

Goulash

Ingredients:

2 lbs. Ground chuck
4 cups Fresh tomatoes chopped
1 cup Onion chopped
2 cups Bell peppers chopped
1 clove Garlic
1/4 cup Parsley chopped
2 cups Elbow macaroni noodles
1 1/2 tablespoons Sugar
Salt & pepper

- Combine beef, peppers, onions, garlic, salt and pepper in a large pot and cook until beef is done and crumbled – drain excess grease
- Add tomatoes and spices and bring to a boil
- Add macaroni, reduce heat and simmer covered stirring occasionally until macaroni is tender
- Add a little water if it starts to get to thick while simmering

Beef Stew

Ingredients:

2 pounds Beef
stew meat
2 pounds Carrots
2 pounds Potatoes
Large Onion
Green Pepper
Salt and pepper
2 tablespoons
Corn Starch
or ¼ cup Flour

- In a pot combine beef, green pepper and onions
- Cook over medium heat until beef is brown
- Add 2 cups of water and simmer for about 45 minutes
- Add carrots and simmer for about 15 minutes
- Add potatoes and enough water to cover all ingredients and simmer until tender
- To thicken add cornstarch or flour to ½ cup of cold water and slowly stir into stew

If we confess our sins, He is faithful and just to forgive us [our] sins, and to cleanse us from all unrighteousness. - 1 John 1:9

Hot Dog Chili

Ingredients:

1 cup water
1/3 cup ketchup
1 lb. ground beef
salt & pepper
onion powder
1 packet taco
seasoning
or
1 tablespoon bulk
taco seasoning
1 teaspoon chili
powder
1 tablespoon sugar
1 tablespoon corn
starch

- Combine beef, salt, pepper and onion powder in a skillet
- Cook until beef is brown and well done
- Drain fat and return skillet to stove
- Combine water and cornstarch
- Add water mixture, ketchup and spices to beef in skillet
- Cook over medium heat, stirring frequently until thick

Hamburger

A good hamburger needs some fat and needs to be thick enough for the bun. I always use 80/20 ground chuck for my hamburgers. Anything leaner makes a dry, tough patty, and any more fat tastes greasy. The best way to cook a burger is on a grill, but a skillet on medium heat will work, and in the winter when you are feeding a crowd, a 350° oven is just the trick. I use between 4 to 6 ounces of meat depending on the type of bun I am using. A hamburger press makes the job of shaping the patties easier, faster and more uniform. I always season my hamburgers with salt, pepper, onion powder and garlic powder. A toasted bun adds flavor and prevents buns from getting soggy. Fresh veggies and real cheese are a must.

Husbands, love your wives, even as Christ also loved the church, and gave himself for it; That he might sanctify and cleanse it with the washing of water by the word. - Ephesians 5:25-26

Hamburger Casserole

Ingredients:
1 lb lean ground beef
1 cup chopped onions
4 cups diced potatoes
1 cup milk
Salt & pepper to taste
4 ounces Provolone cheese (or any cheese you like)
1 teaspoon of corn starch to thicken
**Optional - 1 cup chopped green bell peppers

- In skillet brown beef, onions and peppers
- Combine cold milk and corn starch
- Add potatoes and milk mixture to skillet and stir to combine
- Top with cheese if you wish, and bake in a 350° oven for 1 hour or until potatoes are tender and casserole is brown

But I say unto you which hear, Love your enemies, do good to them which hate you, - Luke 6:27

Cheese Steak Sandwich

Ingredients:

Bun(s) of your choice
1/2 of a medium onion
1/2 of a medium bell pepper
8 oz. of thinly sliced beef
3 or 4 slices of your favorite cheese
Salt & pepper to taste

- Cut the sliced beef into strips
- Slice the onions and peppers
- Combine beef, onions, peppers, salt and pepper in skillet on medium heat
- Cook until vegetables are tender to suit your taste
- Butter bun and toast under broiler or in skillet on stove
- Add beef mixture and cheese to toasted bun

We love Him, because He first loved us. - 1 John 4:19

Ham and Cheese Pinwheels

Ingredients:

Tortilla
Thin sliced Ham
Thin sliced
Turkey
Cream cheese
Shredded Cheese

- **Spread soft cream cheese on tortilla**
- **Sprinkle with shredded cheese**
- **Top with a single layer of meat**
- **Carefully roll into a tight roll leaving a little cream cheese on the edge of the tortilla to seal the roll**
- **Slice into ½ inch slices**

Confess [your] faults one to another, and pray one for another, that ye may be healed. The effectual fervent prayer of a righteous man availeth much. – James 5:16

BBQ Pork Sandwiches

Ingredients:

Pork Loin
Salt & Pepper
2 tablespoons
Onion Powder
¼ cup Lemon
Juice
¼ cup Honey
BBQ Sauce

- Cut pork loin into 1 inch slices
- In a very large pot combine pork, salt, pepper, lemon juice, honey and onion powder
- Start on medium heat
- After about ½ hour reduce heat to medium low, cover and cook for several hours, stirring occasionally, until pork is tender and completely falling apart
- Add BBQ sauce and cook for at least an additional hour

Give to every man that asketh of thee; and of him that taketh away thy goods ask them not again. - Luke 6:30

Chicken Broth and Chicken

Ingredients:

4 lbs. bone in - skin - on chicken.
3 cups water
2 tablespoons butter
2 to 3 teaspoons onion powder or
1 chopped onion
1 to 2 tablespoons honey
2 tablespoon lemon juice
Salt & pepper taste
Any other spices you chose

- In a large pot on medium heat add butter, chicken, onion powder, honey, lemon, salt and pepper
- Cook until chicken is tender and golden brown
- Add water, bring to boil, reduce heat and simmer covered for at least 1 hour
- At this point chicken and broth are ready to be used in recipes
- It can be used immediately or frozen, canned or refrigerated for later use

Come unto me, all ye that labour and are heavy laden, and
I will give you rest. - Matthew 11:28

Chicken Pot Pie

Ingredients:

2 cups cooked, diced chicken
2 cups chicken broth
1 1/2 cups diced potatoes
1 cup diced carrots
1 cup sweet green peas
2 tablespoons flour
salt, pepper, celery seeds, all to taste
1 tablespoon onion powder
2 to 3 pie crusts

- In a pot, combine all ingredients except crust and cook over medium low heat until vegetables are tender
- While filling is cooking, line pie pan, skillet, muffin tins or other oven safe pan with pie crust
- Pour filling into prepared crust
- Top with additional crust, seal edges and cut slits in top crust for venting
- Bake in a preheated 350° oven for 45 to 50 minutes until golden brown and bubbling

And the Lord direct your hearts into the love of God, and into the patient waiting for Christ. - 2 Thessalonians 3:5

Chicken Salad

Ingredients:

1 cup cooked, diced chicken
1/4 cup mayonnaise
1/4 cup pickle relish
2 to 3 teaspoons lemon juice
1 teaspoon sugar
2 to 3 teaspoons onion powder
Salt and pepper to taste

- Shred chicken
- Combine all ingredients in a bowl and mix thoroughly
- Can be served on sandwiches or crackers
- Can be combined with 2 cups of cooked pasta, more or less
- Canned chicken can be used in this recipe

Jesus said unto him, If thou wilt be perfect, go and sell that thou hast, and give to the poor, and thou shalt have treasure in heaven: and come and follow me. - Matthew 19:21

Creamy Chicken Soup

Ingredients:

3 whole chicken
breasts (see Chicken
and Broth page 29)
1 pound raw carrots
1 pound raw potatoes
1 cup milk
3 tablespoons flour
or
1 1/2 tablespoon corn
starch
8 ounces cream
cheese
1 to 2 tablespoons
onion powder
salt and pepper to
taste

- Prepare chicken from page 29
- Remove chicken from bone and dice
- Wash vegetables and dice
- In pot combine strained broth, diced vegetables and chicken
- Cook over medium heat until vegetables are tender
- Add onion powder, salt and pepper
- Combine cold milk with flour or cornstarch
- Add cream cheese and milk mixture to soup
- Stir and heat until thick

Chicken and Dumplings For Granny's Little Dumpling

Prepare one batch of chicken and broth from page 29. Remove chicken from bones and chop. Make sure no small bones remain in pot and return chicken to pot of broth.

Ingredients for Dumplings:
1 ½ cups all-purpose flour · 1 tablespoon baking powder · ½ teaspoon salt · ¾ cup milk

In a bowl combine dry ingredients for dumplings. When broth and chicken has returned to boil and is ready to add dumplings, stir milk into dry dumpling ingredients and mix just until combined. Dip spoon in pot of broth and quickly scoop spoons of dumpling dough into boiling broth, dipping spoon in broth each time and cover pot. Simmer for 12 minutes and enjoy with your favorite little dumpling.

Egg Salad

Ingredients:

6 Hard boiled eggs
3 Tablespoons of real mayonnaise
1 Tablespoon of yellow mustard
1 Tablespoon of sweet pickle relish
Salt and pepper to taste

- Peel eggs
- In a bowl mash eggs with potato masher or fork
- Add remaining ingredients to bowl and mix until well combined
- Best if refrigerated for at least 30 minutes before serving

[38] Give, and it shall be given unto you; good measure, pressed down, and shaken together, and running over, shall men give into your bosom. For with the same measure that ye mete withal it shall be measured to you again. [39] And he spake a parable unto them, Can the blind lead the blind? shall they not both fall into the ditch? [40] The disciple is not above his master: but every one that is perfect shall be as his master. Luke 6

Salmon Patties

Ingredients:

1 can of pink salmon
1 egg
1/4 cup of chopped onions
5 saltine crackers
optional 1/4 cup of chopped green bell peppers
pepper to taste
Butter to fry it in

- Drain salmon
- Crush crackers
- In a bowl lightly beat egg and combine all ingredients
- Form into about 6 patties and let rest for at least 15 minutes
- Put butter in skillet on medium heat
- When pan is hot add patties and cook until golden brown on both sides for approximately 5 to 7 minutes per side

And he saith unto them, Follow me, and I will make you fishers of men. - Matthew 4:19

Potato Soup

Ingredients:

4 cups diced
potatoes
1 cup grated
carrots
1 cup diced
onions
4 tablespoons
real butter
2 cups water
2 cups milk
1 teaspoon salt
1/2 teaspoon
pepper

- Combine onions and butter in pot
- Cook over medium heat until onions are tender and butter is slightly brown
- Add potatoes, carrots and water to pot
- Bring to a boil on medium heat, reduce heat, cover and simmer for 45 minutes
- Add milk, salt and pepper to pot
- Return to medium heat, cook stirring frequently as you break up potato chunks until soup is hot and thick

Creamy Vegetable Soup

Ingredients:

20 oz. Frozen vegetables (California mix)
1 Medium russet potato
12 oz. Evaporated milk
1 Stick butter (1/2 cup)
1 Tablespoon of onion powder
1 Tablespoon of sugar
1 Teaspoon of salt
1/2 Teaspoon of pepper
Enough water to cover the vegetables in the pot

- Peel potato and dice into small pieces
- In a pot combine potato, frozen vegetables, spices and enough water to cover ingredients
- Bring to a boil on medium heat then reduce heat and simmer until vegetables are very tender
- Use a potato masher or an immersion blender to puree vegetables
- Add milk and butter to creamed vegetables and heat, stirring frequently until hot and thick
- You may add cheese of your choice or sour cream when serving

Creamy Alfredo Sauce

Ingredients:

2 cups Heavy
cream
1/2 cup Butter
1 cup Parmesan
cheese
1 cup Mozzarella
cheese
1 clove Garlic
1/4 cup Fresh
Parsley
Salt & pepper

- Put garlic in pan on medium heat and cook stirring until toasted
- Add butter to pan and stir until butter is melted and hot
- Add cream to pan quickly while stirring
- Cook stirring constantly until pan is boiling and mixture thickens
- Add cheese and stir until melted
- Remove from heat, adjust salt and pepper to taste and all a little parsley for color
- Enjoy over pasta, chicken, seafood...

And now abideth faith, hope, charity, these three; but the greatest of these is charity. - 1 Corinthians 13:13

Pork roast

Ingredients:

2 pounds Pork Loin

2 Tablespoons Lemon juice

2 Tablespoons Real honey

Chopped Onion

2 pounds Potatoes

1 ½ pounds Carrots

2 tablespoon Cornstarch

Salt and pepper

- Combine pork, lemon, honey, onion, salt and pepper in large baking dish and cover tightly with foil
- Place in a pre-heated 350° oven for several hours until pork is tender
- Add carrots and potatoes to pan, cut potatoes larger than carrots because they cook faster, recover pan and return to oven until veggies are tender
- Mix cornstarch with ½ cup of cold water and add to pan and return to oven until pan returns to boil

Hobo Meal

Ingredients:

3 or 4 Chicken
tenders
1/2 Medium onion
1 cup Chunked up
New potato
1 cup Baby
carrots
2 tablespoons
Butter
Lemon juice,
honey, salt,
pepper to taste

- Layer ingredients in order listed on a large sheet of heavy duty foil
- Fold foil and seal securely
- Place on preheated grill or on coals from fire
- Cook until ingredients are tender, between 30 minutes to 1 hour depending on fire temperature, turning occasionally
- May also be baked in a 350° oven or skillet on the stove top

Now faith is the substance of things hoped for, the evidence of things not seen. - Hebrews 11:1

Baked Chicken

Ingredients:

4 lbs. - Boneless, skinless chicken breasts
2 tablespoons Honey
2 tablespoons Lemon
Onion powder
Salt & pepper

- Preheat oven to 350°
- Place chicken in an oven safe pan
- Sprinkle with salt, pepper and onion powder
- Flip chicken over, drizzle lemon juice and honey over chicken, then sprinkle with salt, pepper and onion powder
- Cover pan with foil and bake until tender, approximately 1 hour
- Uncover chicken and bake until golden brown

No man hath seen God at any time. If we love one another, God dwelleth in us, and His love is perfected in us. - 1 John 4:12

Fried Pork Chops

Ingredients:

Pork chops
Onion powder
Salt & pepper
A little bit of oil

- Sprinkle spices on both sides of pork chops
- Heat skillet with small amount of oil on medium heat
- When skillet is hot add seasoned chops and cook until tender and golden brown on both sides

[8] Will a man rob God? Yet ye have robbed me. But ye say, Wherein have we robbed thee? In tithes and offerings. [9] Ye are cursed with a curse: for ye have robbed me, even this whole nation. [10] Bring ye all the tithes into the storehouse, that there may be meat in mine house, and prove me now herewith, saith the LORD of hosts, if I will not open you the windows of heaven, and pour you out a blessing, that there shall not be room enough to receive it. [11] And I will rebuke the devourer for your sakes, and he shall not destroy the fruits of your ground; neither shall your vine cast her fruit before the time in the field, saith the LORD of hosts. - Malachi 3

Fried Chicken Tenders

Ingredients:
6 chicken tenders
1 sleeve of Townhouse or Ritz crackers
1 egg
1 tablespoon honey
1 tablespoon lemon juice
1 teaspoon onion powder
Salt & pepper
Oil for frying

- Combine egg, honey, lemon, onion powder, salt and pepper
- Put chicken in bowl with lid and pour egg mixture over chicken then place in fridge for an hour or longer to marinate
- Crush crackers up fine and pour out on plate
- Place chicken tenders one at a time in crumbs and press out flat with fork while coating with crumbs
- Let coated chicken rest for about 15 minutes then place single layer in hot pan filled with about ¼ inch of oil
- Cook until brown and crisp on both sides

Swedish Meatballs Recipe

Ingredients:

Frozen meatballs
1 cup Sour cream
1 cup Cream
2 tablespoons
Worcestershire
sauce
Salt, pepper and
onion powder

- Combine all ingredients in crock pot and stir until well combined
- Heat on high until sauce begins to bubble stirring occasionally
- Reduce to low heat and cook at least 2 hours
- Taste and adjust spices to taste
- Leave crock pot on low or warm setting and add to the party buffet

Make a joyful noise unto the LORD, all ye lands.[2] Serve the LORD with gladness: come before his presence with singing.[3] Know ye that the LORD he is God: it is he that hath made us, and not we ourselves; we are his people, and the sheep of his pasture.[4] Enter into his gates with thanksgiving, and into his courts with praise: be thankful unto him, and bless his name.[5] For the LORD is good; his mercy is everlasting; and his truth endureth to all generations.- Psalm 100

Chicken and Rice

Ingredients:

1 lb. Chicken tenders
1 medium onion
4 tablespoons Real Butter
1 tablespoon Lemon juice
1 tablespoon honey
1 cup long grain rice
2 cups water
Salt & pepper

- In skillet on medium heat combine 2 tablespoons butter, chicken, chopped onion, lemon, honey, salt and pepper
- Cook until chicken is golden brown and tender
- Add 2 cups of water to skillet and heat until boiling
- When water is at full boil add 2 cups of long grain rice
- Cover and reduce heat to low once pan returns to boil
- Cook without removing lid for 20 minutes
- Remove lid stir rice and adjust salt and pepper to taste and add remaining butter

Ham & Cheese Omelet

Ingredients:

3 eggs
2 slices cheese
1/3 bell pepper
1 small onion
1/2 cup diced ham
Salt & pepper

- In skillet on medium heat combine butter, ham, peppers and onion cook until slightly tender
- In small bowl beat eggs until slightly foamy, add salt and pepper
- Add eggs to skillet and cover
- Cook until eggs start to set and flip omelet in skillet
- Add cheese to top of omelet
- Once eggs are firm fold omelet in half and serve hot

And when ye stand praying, forgive, if ye have ought against any: that your Father also which is in heaven may forgive you your trespasses. [26]But if ye do not forgive, neither will your Father which is in heaven forgive your trespasses. - Mark 11:25

Oven Bacon

Ingredients:

Thick Bacon

- Place bacon in a single layer on cookie sheet
- Place in a preheated 400° oven for 15 to 20 minutes or until done and crisp
- Flip half way through cooking

18 And he saith unto them, Are ye so without understanding also? Do ye not perceive, that whatsoever thing from without entereth into the man, it cannot defile him; 19 Because it entereth not into his heart, but into the belly, and goeth out into the draught, purging all meats? - Mark 7

Scrambled Eggs

Ingredients:

Eggs
Salt
Pepper
Butter

- **Put butter in skillet and heat on medium heat**
- **In a bowl combine eggs, salt and pepper, mix until foamy**
- **Add eggs to preheated skillet**
- **Stir eggs frequently making sure to remove all cooked eggs from bottom of skillet**
- **Continue to cook until eggs are firm**

[24] This is the day which the LORD hath made; we will rejoice and be glad in it. [25] Save now, I beseech thee, O LORD: O LORD, I beseech thee, send now prosperity. [26] Blessed be he that cometh in the name of the LORD: we have blessed you out of the house of the LORD. - Psalm 118

Buttermilk Pancakes

Ingredients:

1 cup All purpose flour

1 tablespoon Sugar

2 teaspoons Baking powder

1/2 teaspoon Salt

1 Egg

1 cup Buttermilk

2 tablespoons Oil

1/2 teaspoon Vanilla

- Combine all wet ingredients in bowl and mix until well combined
- Add dry ingredients all at once and lightly mix, small lumps are okay
- Let batter rest for at least 15 minutes
- Preheat pan with small amount of butter on medium heat
- Lightly stir pancake batter
- Scoop approximately ¼ cup of batter into center of skillet
- Cook until bubbles pop on surface
- Flip pancake and cook until slightly brown on bottom side

Chocolate Gravy

Ingredients:

1 cup sugar
2 tablespoons cocoa powder
1/2 cup flour (or 1/4 cup corn starch for Gluten free)
2 cups milk
2 tablespoons butter
1 teaspoon vanilla extract

- Mix dry ingredients in pot
- Slowly add milk
- Cook over medium heat, stirring constantly, until thick
- Add butter
- Remove from heat and pour over hot biscuits or pancakes

If a man say, I love God, and hateth his brother, he is a liar: for he that loveth not his brother whom he hath seen, how can he love God whom he hath not seen? - 1 John 4:20

Sausage Gravy

Ingredients:

Sausage
¼ cup Flour
2 cups Milk
Salt & Pepper
to taste

- In skillet where sausage was prepared leave small amount of grease and break up a small amount of sausage if desired
- Adjust heat to medium
- Add flour, salt and pepper, cook stirring constantly until flour and grease are well combined
- Add milk all at once, cook until boiling and thick, stirring constantly
- If gravy is too thick a little more milk can be added
- If gravy is too thin, cook a few minutes longer, but don't add more flour

BBQ Little Smokies - Sweet & Spicy

Ingredients:

**Little Smokies
Sausages
1/3 cup BBQ sauce
1/3 cup Grape jelly**

- **In a crock pot add all ingredients and stir until combined**
- **Heat on high stirring occasionally until bubbling**
- **Reduce heat to low and sit on party buffet**

1Children, obey your parents in the Lord: for this is right.

2Honour thy father and mother;

(which is the first commandment with promise;)

3That it may be well with thee, and thou mayest live long on the earth. - Ephesians 6

Sweet Potato Fries

Ingredients:

Sweet potatoes -
3 medium
Salt to taste
Cinnamon to taste
1 tablespoon of
grape seed oil

- Cut potatoes into ¼ inch square strips or thicker if desired
- Combine all ingredients
- Mix until potatoes are well coated
- Spread on cookie sheet and bake in 400° oven, flipping occasionally until tender and golden brown

My son, forget not my law; but let thine heart keep my commandnents: ² For length of days, and long life, and peace, shall they add to thee. ³ Let not mercy and truth forsake thee: bind them about thy neck; write them upon the table of thine heart:⁴ So shalt thou find favour and good understanding in the sight of God and man.⁵ Trust in the LORD with all thine heart; and lean not unto thine own understanding.⁶ In all thy ways acknowledge him, and he shall direct thy paths. - Proverbs 3

Pumpkin Cheese Ball

Ingredients:

8 oz. Shredded
cheddar cheese
8 oz. Cream
cheese
1/4 Cup Pumpkin
1/4 Cup Pineapple
preserves
1/2 Teaspoon
Pumpkin pie spice

- Mix all ingredients in bowl until well combined
- Shape into balls
- Place in fridge until firm
- Serve with crackers of your choice

Delight thyself also in the Lord:
and he shall give thee the desires of thine heart.
Psalm 37:4

Fried Squash

Ingredients:

2 summer squash
1/4 cup of
cornmeal
2 teaspoons of
sugar
Salt & pepper to
taste
Oil for frying

- Wash squash and slice thin about ¼ inch thick
- Combine cornmeal, sugar, salt and pepper in a bag or bowl with a lid
- Add squash to other ingredients and toss until squash is coated
- Remove coated squash and place on rack or plate to rest
- Add about ¼ inch of oil to pan
- Cook on medium heat
- Add squash to pan once oil is hot
- Cook 5 to 7 minutes per side until both sides are brown

Potato Pancakes

Ingredients:

2 cups of leftover
mashed potatoes
1 egg
3/4 cup of flour
1/2 cup to 1 cup
 of milk
Salt, pepper and
onion powder to
taste.

- Combine flour, baking powder, salt, pepper and onion powder
- Add egg, milk and mix until combined.
- Add potatoes, mix until smooth
- In a skillet on medium heat add butter or oil to fry
- Once pan is hot, scoop approximately ¼ cup portions of batter into pan
- Fry until golden brown on both sides, approximately 5 to 7 minutes per side

And heal the sick that are therein, and say unto them, The kingdom of God is come nigh unto you. - Luke 10:9

Onion Rings

Ingredients:
Vidalia or sweet
onions
1/3 cup corn starch
3/4 cup all purpose
flour
1 egg
1 tablespoon
baking powder
1 tablespoon sugar
1 teaspoon salt
1/2 teaspoon
pepper
3/4 cup milk or
buttermilk
Oil to cook

- Slice onions approximately ¼ inch thick and separate rings
- In a bag or bowl with a lid, combine cornstarch and sliced onions. Shake until well coated
- In bowl combine all remaining ingredients and any cornstarch that did not stick to onion rings, mix well to make batter
- Pour about ½ an inch of oil in a skillet and preheat on medium heat
- Once oil is hot, dip onion rings in batter and carefully place a single layer of onion rings in hot oil
- Cook turning at least once, until golden brown on both sides and drain on rack

Hash Browns

Ingredients:

Firm taters like
Red Skin or Yukon
Gold work best
Salt and pepper
Butter for frying

- Peel and grate potatoes
- Wash until all visible starch is removed
- Dry potatoes well
- Put butter in a pan on medium heat
- When pan is hot, add potatoes, salt and pepper to taste
- Fry until golden brown

[31] Whether therefore ye eat, or drink, or whatsoever ye do, do all to the glory of God. [32] Give none offence, neither to the Jews, nor to the Gentiles, nor to the church of God: [33] Even as I please all men in   all things, not seeking mine own profit, but the profit of many, that they may be saved. - 1 Corinthians 10

New Potatoes and Green Beans

Ingredients:

Fresh green beans Fresh New potatoes
Real butter
Salt and pepper

- **Wash beans and potatoes well**
- **String and break beans**
- **Put beans, whole potatoes, butter, salt and pepper, and enough water to cover beans and potatoes in a pot**
- **Bring to a boil on the stove, reduce heat and simmer until done and tender**

7 Be not deceived; God is not mocked: for whatsoever a man soweth, that shall he also reap.8 For he that soweth to his flesh shall of the flesh reap corruption; but he that soweth to the Spirit shall of the Spirit reap life everlasting.9 And let us not be weary in well doing: for in due season we shall reap, if we faint not. - Galatians 6

Fried Potatoes with Onions

Ingredients:

Yukon Gold
and/or Red skin
potatoes Onion
Grape seed oil
Salt & pepper

- Wash potatoes well (peel if you wish) and dice
- Chop onion
- In a pan on medium heat, add oil or butter
- Once pan is hot, add potatoes
- Stir frequently with a stiff spatula, scraping the bottom of the pan
- Once potatoes have started to cook, add onions
- Cook until golden brown and well done

Who his own self bare our sins in his own body on the tree, that we, being dead to sins, should live unto righteousness: by whose stripes ye were healed. - 1 Peter 2:24

Buttermilk Ranch Dressing

Ingredients:

1/2 cup Buttermilk
1/3 cup Mayonnaise
1/3 cup Sour cream
2 tablespoons
Lemon juice
2 tablespoons
Honey
2 teaspoons Dried
parsley
1 teaspoon Onion
powder
1/2 teaspoon Salt
1/2 teaspoon garlic
powder
1/8 teaspoon Pepper
1/8 teaspoon Dill
1/8 teaspoon
Paprika

- Combine all ingredients in mason jar or other container with tight fitting lid
- Shake until well combined. Emersion blender or small hand mixer may also be used to combine ingredients
- May be stored in the refrigerator until date on buttermilk used in dressing

Hatred stirreth up strifes: but
love covereth all sins.
Proverbs 10:12

Bacon & Bleu Cheese Wedge Salad

Ingredients:

Iceberg lettuce
Bacon
Bleu cheese
dressing Tomato
Hard boiled eggs
Shredded
cheddar cheese
Crumbled bleu
cheese

- Clean and quarter a head of iceberg lettuce
- Dice tomato and egg
- Crumble bacon
- Place lettuce on plate, drizzle with dressing, arrange tomato and egg on beside of lettuce
- Top with bacon, shredded cheese and blue cheese

But when thou doest alms, let not thy left hand know what thy right hand doeth: That thine alms may be in secret: and thy Father which seeth in secret himself shall reward thee openly.
Matthew 6:3-4

Recipe and photo by Samantha Mullins

Potato Salad

Ingredients:

2 lbs. Taters
4 Boiled eggs
1/2 cup
Mayonnaise
1/3 cup
Mustard 1/2
cup Pickle
relish
Onion powder
Salt and pepper

- Place whole unpeeled potatoes and eggs in a large pot, cover with water
- Bring to a boil on the stove, reduce heat to a simmer and boil until potatoes are tender
- Once potatoes are tender, drain and rinse with cold water
- While potatoes and eggs are still warm, peel them (this is the easiest way)
- Mash warm eggs and break potatoes into small pieces
- In a small bowl combine mayo, mustard, pickle relish, onion powder, salt and pepper
- Pour mayo dressing over potatoes and eggs, mix until combined
- Best if refrigerated one hour before serving

Pinto Beans

Ingredients:

Dry pinto beans
Salt to taste
Pepper to taste
Filtered Water

Optional:
Fatback
Salt pork
Bacon grease
Bacon
Onion

- Wash beans well
- Add enough water to cover beans twice
- Soak overnight or put on stove and bring to a boil for ten minutes and soak for one hour
- After soaking, rinse beans again
- Add enough water to cover one inch above beans
- Add salt and pepper
- Return pan to stove, bring to a boil, reduce heat, simmer until well done a few hours
- If you wish to season with fat or meat, it should be added after soaking when you begin to cook the beans

Easy Mac & Cheese

Ingredients:

8 oz. Cheddar
cheese
2 1/2 cups Milk
3 tablespoons Flour
4 tablespoons Real
butter
Salt and pepper to
taste
8 oz. Uncooked
macaroni (2 cups)

- Cook macaroni according to package directions and drain
- In a bowl combine milk, flour, salt and pepper
- Combine all ingredients in pot and return to stove over medium heat
- Cook stirring constantly until cheese is melted and sauce is bubbling and thick

Grandchildren are the crown of old men, And the glory of
sons is their fathers. - Proverbs 17:6

Fried Green Tomatoes

Ingredients:
3 Totally green tomatoes
1 cup Self rising flour
1 Egg
1 cup Buttermilk
1 to 2 cups Yellow corn meal
1 cup - Oil
Salt and pepper to taste
Optional
Sugar

- Slice tomatoes about ¼ inch thick and place on rack and salt to allow excess moisture to drip off
- Put flour in one bowl, egg and buttermilk in a second bowl, and cornmeal and sugar in a third bowl
- Dry tomatoes with paper towel, salt and pepper each side and dip in each bowl in the order listed until coated
- Return to rack and allow to sit for about 15 minutes
- Preheat oil in pan on medium heat, add tomatoes to hot oil and fry until golden brown on each side

Corn Fritters

Ingredients:

2 cups Fresh corn
1 cup All purpose flour
2 teaspoons Baking powder
1 1/2 tablespoons Melted butter
1/2 teaspoon Salt
1 teaspoon Sugar
1 - Egg
1/2 to 1 cup Milk
Oil to fry in

- Cut corn off cob and scrape cob
- Combine flour, baking powder, salt and sugar
- Add egg and milk, mix well
- Stir in corn until well mixed
- In a pan on medium heat add butter
- Once pan is hot, scoop approximately ¼ cup portions of batter into pan
- Cook until golden brown on both sides approximately 5 to 7 minutes on each side

Nevertheless I tell you the truth; It is expedient for you that I go away: for if I go not away, the Comforter will not come unto you; but if I depart, I will send him unto you. - **John 16:7**

Cornbread Stuffing/Dressing

- Put butter in skillet or other baking dish, place in oven and preheat to 350°
- Crumble cornbread
- In a large bowl add eggs, beat slightly, add broth, onions, celery, and spices, mix until combined
- Fold in cornbread crumbs until well coated
- Once butter is hot, pour into the stuffing mixture and fold in
- Put stuffing in skillet or baking dish and return to oven
- Bake for one hour or until set and golden brown

Owe no man any thing, but to love one another: for he that loveth another hath fulfilled the law. - Romans 13:8

Ingredients:

Batch of Hillbilly Kitchen Cornbread (page 78 or 79)
2 to 2 1/2 cups chicken or turkey broth
1 cup chopped onions
1 cup chopped celery
1/2 cup real butter
3 eggs
1 tablespoon rubbed sage
2 teaspoons parsley
1 teaspoon thyme
Salt and pepper to taste

The LORD is my shepherd; I shall not want.[2] He maketh me to lie down in green pastures: he leadeth me beside the still waters.[3] He restoreth my soul: he leadeth me in the paths of righteousness for his name's sake.[4] Yea, though I walk through the valley of the shadow of death, I will fear no evil: for thou art with me; thy rod and thy staff they comfort me.[5] Thou preparest a table before me in the presence of mine enemies: thou anointest my head with oil; my cup runneth over.[6] Surely goodness and mercy shall follow me all the days of my life: and I will dwell in the house of the LORD for ever. - Psalm 23

Cole Slaw

Ingredients:

1/2 head cabbage
1 medium carrot
1/2 cup mayo
1/3 to 1/2 cup milk
1 tablespoon vinegar
1 1/2 tablespoons
 lemon juice
2 to 3 tablespoons sugar
1 tablespoon onion powder
salt & pepper to taste
2 tablespoons**optional**
buttermilk powder

- Grate cabbage and carrot
- Combine mayonnaise, milk, vinegar, lemon, sugar, onion powder, salt, pepper
- Mix well
- Pour the mayo dressing over cabbage and carrot
- Mix well
- Best if refrigerated at least one hour before serving

He coveteth greedily all the day long:
but the righteous giveth and spareth not. - Proverbs 21:26

Corn Pudding

Ingredients:

3 1/2 to 4 cups
fresh corn
4 eggs
1/4 cup real butter
2 to 4 tablespoons
sugar
1 cup cream or
milk
1 tablespoon of
baking powder
3 tablespoons corn
starch
1/2 teaspoon salt

- Cut corn off cob and scrape cob well
- In a large bowl add eggs and beat slightly
- Add all ingredients to eggs and mix well
- Pour ingredients into greased oven safe pan
- Bake in 350° oven for 45 minutes to 1 hour until set and golden brown

And the Lord direct your hearts
into the love of God, and into the
patient waiting for Christ.
2 Thessalonians 3:5

Old Fashioned Buttermilk Biscuits

Ingredients: 2 cups all purpose flour · 1 tablespoon baking powder · ½ teaspoon salt · 1/3 cup butter · 1 tablespoon of honey · ¾ cup of buttermilk

Granny always made buttermilk biscuits for breakfast. Sometimes we didn't have bacon or sausage or even eggs to go with them, but buttermilk biscuits with Granny's real honey and fresh churned butter were always a treat. I watched her make them so many times I can still see her standing in her kitchen in her faded apron and hands covered in flour making a big pan of biscuits. First she sifted the flour, baking powder and salt into her bowl. Then she cut in her freshly churned butter. She added her fresh honey to her buttermilk. She gave it a little stir then poured it in the flour and butter mixture. She threw a little flour down on her table so the dough didn't stick to the table and then she rolled out the dough and cut it into round biscuits about 1/2 inch high. After sitting in the wood stove oven that she got really hot (415 degrees Fahrenheit) for 15 minutes, the biscuits had risen to a few inches high and they were golden brown.

Biscuits Made With Oil

Ingredients:

2 cups self rising flour
1/3 cup oil
3/4 cup milk

Forbearing one another, and forgiving one another, if any man have a quarrel against any: even as Christ forgave you, so also [do] ye.
Colossians 3:13

- **Combine all ingredients in bowl and mix lightly until dry ingredients are moist**
- **Turn onto a well floured surface**
- **Knead lightly only until dough is firm enough to cut**
- **Roll or press out until ¾ to 1 inch thick**
- **Cut into 2 or 3 inch circles**
- **Place biscuits on pan about ½ inch apart**
- **Let biscuits rest about 15 minutes before baking**
- **Bake in 450° oven for 15 minutes until biscuits are golden brown**

Butter Biscuits

Ingredients:

2 cups Self rising flour
1/3 cup Real butter
3/4 cup Milk

- In a bowl combine flour and butter by cutting butter into flour with fork or pastry blade until mixture resembles small crumbs
- Add milk and stir lightly just until dry ingredients are moist
- Turn onto a well floured surface
- Knead lightly only folding 3 or 4 times
- Roll or press out until ¾ to 1 inch thick
- Cut into 2 or 3 inch circles
- Place biscuits on pan about ½ inch apart
- Let biscuits rest about 15 minutes before baking
- Bake in 450° oven for 15 minutes until biscuits are golden brown

He that loveth not knoweth not God; for God is love.-1 John 4:8

Mayonnaise Rolls

Ingredients:

1 cup of self
rising flour (or 1
cup all-purpose
flour + 1/2
tablespoon
baking powder +
1/4 teaspoon
salt)
3 tablespoons of
mayonnaise
1 teaspoon of
sugar
1/2 cup of milk

- Combine all ingredients in a
  bowl and mix until moist.
  Do not over mix
- Spoon into six greased muffin
  cups
- Bake in pre-heated 425° oven
  for 15 minutes
- For best results let rest in
  muffin pan for about 15
  minutes before baking

Old Fashioned Apple Butter

Ingredients for 8 pints :

8 to 10 lbs. apples
 2 cups brown sugar
2 cups white sugar
1 cup juice or water (I used apple cider)
2 teaspoons vanilla
1 tablespoon cinnamon
1 teaspoon cloves
1 1/2 teaspoons nutmeg
2 teaspoons salt
***All spices will have to be adjusted to taste

- Wash apples and cut into chunks removing core
- Combine apples and all other ingredients in a large pot
- Heat over medium low heat, stirring occasionally until pot reaches a boil
- Reduce heat to low and cook for approximately 8 hours, stirring occasionally
- If necessary use potato masher or a emersion blender to smooth apple butter
- Adjust spices to suit taste
- Process in a water bath canner to preserve
- May also be cooked in a crock pot or programmable cooker

Johnny Cakes

Ingredients:

1 cup yellow cornmeal
1/4 cup hot water
1/4 cup buttermilk
3/4 teaspoon salt
1 1/2 teaspoons baking powder
1 1/2 teaspoons sugar
1 egg
Butter or bacon grease to cook it in

- Combine dry ingredients in bowl
- Add egg and buttermilk, stir until moist
- Add hot water, stir until combined
- Preheat pan on medium heat with bacon grease or butter
- Scoop approximately ¼ cup portions of batter into pan
- Cook until golden brown on both sides and completely done in the center, approximately 5 to 7 minutes per side
- Reduce heat if necessary
- For best results let batter sit for 15 minutes before cooking

Buttermilk Cornbread

Ingredients:

1 cup All purpose flour

1 cup Corn meal

1/4 teaspoon Salt

1 teaspoon Baking soda

2 teaspoons Baking powder

2 Eggs

1 cup Buttermilk

1/4 cup Real butter

2 tablespoons Real honey

- Put butter in skillet or baking pan and place in oven
- Turn oven on 400° to preheat oven and skillet
- Combine dry ingredients in bowl
- Add egg, buttermilk and honey, stir until moist
- Remove hot pan from oven and pour hot butter into batter, stir until combined
- Pour batter into hot pan and return to oven bake 20 to 25 minutes until golden brown
- Use 8 or 10 inch skillet or will make 12 muffins

Basic Cornbread

Ingredients:

2 cups self rising
corn meal mix
1 egg
1 1/3 cups milk
1/4 cup butter
2 tablespoons
real honey

- Put butter in skillet or baking pan and place in oven
- Turn oven on 400° to preheat oven and skillet
- Combine dry ingredients in bowl
- Add egg, buttermilk and honey, stir until moist
- Remove hot pan from oven and pour hot butter into batter, stir until combined
- Pour batter into hot pan and return to oven, bake 20 to 25 minutes until golden brown
- Use 8 or 10 inch skillet or will make 12 muffins

Hardtack

Ingredients:

3 cups of all purpose flour
2 teaspoons of salt
1 cup of water

- Combine flour and salt then mix in water
- Roll dough out on wax paper to about ¼ inch thick
- Poke holes in dough every ½ inch – a dough docker for pizza crusts works well for this process
- Cut dough into 3 or 4 in. squares
- Bake in a 250° oven for 8 hours or until hard and dry
- Turn ½ way through baking and every ½ hour after 8 hours until done
- Stored indefinitely in vacuum sealed container

Banana Nut Muffins

Ingredients:

4 or 5 bananas
2 Cups all purpose flour
1/2 Cup Chopped pecans
1 Tablespoon Baking powder
1/2 Teaspoon Cinnamon
1/2 Cup Ground Flax seed
1 Cup Sugar
1 Stick Real butter
2 Eggs
1 Teaspoon vanilla
1/2 Teaspoon Salt

- Combine bananas and sugar in bowl and cream with mixer
- Add soft butter, eggs and vanilla, mix until combined
- Combine flour, baking powder, salt, cinnamon and flax seed
- Fold dry ingredients and nuts into banana mixture
- Divide mixture into lined muffin cups, filling cups approximately ¾ full
- Bake in preheated 375° oven for approximately 20 minutes
- Makes 12 muffins

Blueberry Muffins

Ingredients:

1/2 cup Real butter
1 cup Sugar
2 Eggs
1 teaspoon Real vanilla extract
2 teaspoons Baking powder
1/4 teaspoon Salt
2 cups All purpose flour
1/2 cup Milk
2 cups blueberries

- Cream butter and sugar until fluffy
- Combine flour, salt and baking powder
- In a bowl, lightly beat eggs
- Add eggs, vanilla and milk to butter mixture
- Fold flour into batter stirring lightly just until combined
- Fold in blueberries carefully
- Scoop into lined muffin pans filling ¾ full
- May be topped with crumb topping before baking
- Bake in preheated 375° oven for 17 to 22 minutes

Cream Cheese Filling

Ingredients:

8 ounces cream cheese
1/4 cup sugar
1 egg
1 to 2 teaspoons real vanilla extract

- Soften cream cheese to room temperature
- Combine all ingredients in bowl until smooth and creamy
- Add to the top or center of muffins, pastries, pies, quick breads, coffee cakes, or cup cakes before baking
- May be stored in the refrigerator for at least a week for future use

Then he said unto them, Go your way, eat the fat, and drink the sweet, and send portions unto them for whom nothing is prepared: for this day is holy unto our Lord: neither be ye sorry; for the joy of the Lord is your strength. - Nehemiah 8:10

Pumpkin Spiced Muffins

Ingredients:

1 1/2 cups all purpose flour
2 teaspoons pumpkin pie spice
1 teaspoon baking powder
1/2 teaspoon baking soda
1/2 teaspoon salt
1/2 cup oil
1/2 cup sugar
1/2 cup brown sugar
2 eggs
1 teaspoon real vanilla extract
1 can pumpkin

sugar & cinnamon topping:
1/4 cup sugar
1 teaspoon cinnamon
1/4 cup melted butter

- Combine flour, baking powder, baking soda and salt
- In a large bowl, beat eggs lightly add oil, sugar and vanilla mix until well combined
- Stir pumpkin into wet ingredients until well combined
- Add dry ingredients into wet ingredients and stir lightly until well combined
- Divide batter in lined muffin cups filling approximately ¾ full
- May be topped with crumb topping or cream cheese filling before baking
- Bake in preheated 375° oven for 17 to 22 minutes
- After baking, may be topped with cinnamon and sugar or cream cheese frosting
- Makes 12 muffins
- For cinnamon & sugar topping, combine cinnamon & sugar, dip top baked muffin in melted butter, then in cinnamon & sugar

Offer unto God thanksgiving; and pay thy vows unto the most High
Psalms 50:14

Crumb Topping

Ingredients:

1/4 cup flour
1/4 cup sugar
2 tablespoons real butter

Optional**
1 teaspoon cinnamon
 2 to 3 tablespoons finely chopped pecans or other nuts

- Combine ingredients in bowl, except nuts, and hand mix with fork or pastry blade until mixture resembles coarse sand or fine gravel
- Do not over mix, butter should not be creamed
- Add nuts after other ingredients have been combined
- crumb topping can be added to muffins, pies, quick breads, coffee cakes, and cup cakes before baking
- May be stored in the refrigerator for a few weeks for future use

Cream Cheese Frosting

Ingredients:

1 Stick of real butter

8 ounce package cream cheese

1 Cup of sugar

1 Teaspoon real vanilla

- Soften cream cheese and butter to room temperature
- Combine ingredients in a large bowl
- Use a mixer and cream ingredients until fluffy and smooth
- I've used it on yellow cake, chocolate cake, pineapple cake, cookies, danishes, cinnamon rolls and it even works as a fruit dip.

A good man out of the good treasure of his heart bringeth forth that which is good; and an evil man out of the evil treasure of his heart bringeth forth that which is evil: for of the abundance of the heart his mouth speaketh. - Luke 6:45

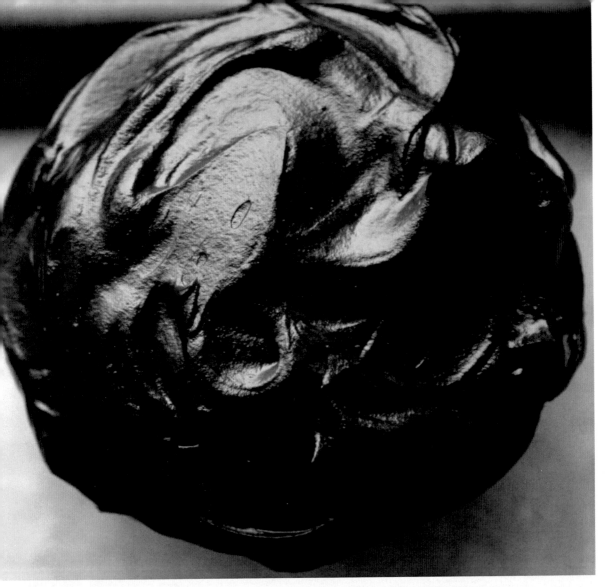

Creamy Chocolate Frosting

Wherefore, my beloved brethren, let every man be swift to hear,
slow to speak, slow to wrath:

James 1:19

Ingredients:

6 tablespoons real butter
6 tablespoons unsweetened, all natural cocoa
2 tablespoons real honey
1 teaspoon real vanilla extract
2 cups powdered sugar
2 to 4 tablespoons milk or cream

- Combine sugar and cocoa
- Mixing by hand add softened butter, honey, vanilla and 2 tablespoons of milk or cream
- Once ingredients are moist a mixer may be used to create a fluffy, creamy, smooth, spreadable frosting
- As you are mixing add additional cream or milk if necessary to create desired consistency being careful not to make frosting too thin

6But this I say, He which soweth sparingly shall reap also sparingly; and he which soweth bountifully shall reap also bountifully.7Every man according as he purposeth in his heart, so let him give; not grudgingly, or of necessity: for God loveth a cheerful giver.8And God is able to make all grace abound toward you; that ye, always having all sufficiency in all things, may abound to every good work:9(As it is written, He hath dispersed abroad; he hath given to the poor: his righteousness remaineth for ever.10Now he that ministereth seed to the sower both minister bread for your food, and multiply your seed sown, and increase the fruits of your righteousness;)11Being enriched in every thing to all bountifulness, which causeth through us thanksgiving to God.

2 Corinthians 9

Butter Cream Frosting

Ingredients:

1/2 cup Soft, real butter
4 cups Powdered sugar
1/2 teaspoon Salt
2 teaspoons Real vanilla
1/4 cup Heavy cream
2 tablespoons White corn syrup

- Mixing by hand, combine all ingredients except one half of cream in a large bowl
- Once ingredients are moist, a mixer may be used to create a fluffy, creamy, smooth, spreadable frosting
- As you are mixing, add additional cream if necessary to create desired consistency being careful not to make frosting too thin

You can use it to frost homemade cookies, cakes and cupcakes, and it's easy to add color to it for decorating. You can spread it with a knife, or you can pipe it on.

Chocolate Fudge Icing

Ingredients:

2 cups Sugar
3 Heaping tablespoons cocoa
2/3 cup Whole milk
1/2 cup Real butter
1 1/2 teaspoons Real vanilla

Recipe by Samantha Mullins

- Bring the first three ingredients to a boil over medium heat in large pot stirring frequently
- Add vanilla and butter stirring constantly from this point
- Once pot returns to a boil, cook stirring constantly for 3 ½ minutes

This icing is not spreadable; you must pour it on your cake while it's still warm. You cannot whip it into a frosting. It is a coating.

There is no fear in love; but perfect love casteth out fear: because fear hath torment. He that feareth is not made perfect in love.
1 John 4:18

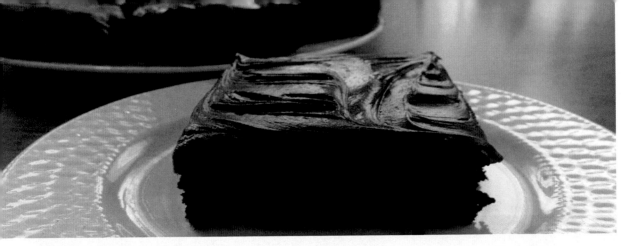

Brownies

Ingredients:

1 cup melted butter
2 cups sugar
2 teaspoons vanilla
4 eggs
3/4 cup cocoa
1 cup all purpose flour
1/2 teaspoon baking powder
1/4 teaspoon salt
Optional**
1 cup milk chocolate chips
1 1/2 cup homemade creamy chocolate frosting (page 88)

- Combine all dry ingredients
- In bowl lightly beat eggs
- Add eggs and butter to flour mixture and mix lightly, just until combined
- Nuts or chocolate chips may be added if desired
- Pour mixture into greased baking pan
- Bake in a 9 x 13 pan @ 350° F. (177° C.) for 30 to 35 minutes
- Frost while still slightly warm

Chocolate Cake

Ingredients:
2 cups Sugar
1 3/4 cup Cake flour
3/4 cup Cocoa powder
1 1/2 teaspoon Baking powder
1 1/2 teaspoon Baking soda
1 teaspoon Salt
1 cup Milk
1/2 cup Oil (grape seed)
2 teaspoons Real vanilla extract
3/4 cup hot water

Recipe and photo by Samantha Mullins

- Combine dry ingredients in a large bowl
- Add lightly beaten eggs, milk, oil and vanilla
- Stir until all ingredients are well combined, a mixer may be used but do not over mix
- Add 3/4 cup of very hot water to batter and stir in by hand
- Put batter in greased baking pans or muffin cups
- Bake in a preheated 350° oven for 45 minutes or until done

Yield-One large Bundt cake or two dozen cupcakes or one 9 x 11 sheet cake

Pineapple Wedding Cake

Ingredients:

4 Eggs
2 Teaspoons Real Vanilla Extract
2 Sticks Butter (1 cup)
2 Cups Sugar
3 Cups Cake Flour or All Purpose Flour
1 Tablespoon Baking Powder
1/2 Teaspoon Salt

- In a pot, combine all ingredients for the filling and cook over medium heat, stirring constantly until mixture boils and thickens, then set aside to cool
- Separate eggs and put whites in large bowl
- In a bowl, combine butter, sugar and vanilla and mix until creamed, then add egg yolks slowly while mixing
- Add baking powder, salt and powdered milk to flour

1/4 Cup Powdered Milk
1 Cup Pineapple Juice

Filling Ingredients:
20 Ounce Can Of Crushed Pineapples (Drained)
1/2 Stick Real Butter
1 Cup Brown Sugar
2 Tablespoons Cornstarch

- Slowly add flour mixture to creamed sugar mixture while mixing until well combined
- Beat egg whites until fluffy and stiff
- Carefully fold egg whites into batter
- Pour ½ of batter into well greased pan
- Add filling
- Pour other ½ of batter over filling
- It will be necessary to spread batter and filling as they are both quite thick
- Bake in a preheated 350° oven for 35 to 45 minutes until done and golden brown
- Allow cake to cool and top with cream cheese frosting

Frost with Cream Cheese Frosting on page 87

This recipe came about when one of my girls wanted a pineapple wedding cake. I tested a few cakes, took bits and pieces of from several recipes and then put my own touches on it. It has become a family favorite for special occasions. That wedding never took place, but the cake has become a part of the family.

"Who so findeth a wife, findeth a good thing,
and obtaineth fauour of the Lord."
Proverbs 18:22

No-Bake Cookies

Ingredients:

1 1/2 to 2 cups sugar
1/4 cup cocoa
1/2 cup cold pressed, unbleached coconut oil or real butter
1/2 cup milk
1 teaspoon real vanilla extract
1 cup peanut butter
3 cups quick oats

Therefore I take pleasure in infirmities, in reproaches, in necessities, in persecutions, in distresses for Christ's sake: for when I am weak, then am I strong. - 2 Corinthians 12:10

- In a pot, combine sugar and cocoa
- Add oil or butter and milk, place pot on medium heat, cook, stirring occasionally until pot reaches a boil
- Continue to cook stirring constantly over medium heat until it reaches about 235° Fahrenheit or soft ball stage. This will take 3 to 5 minutes
- Remove from heat, stir in vanilla and peanut butter, mix until smooth
- Add oatmeal mix until well combined
- Drop spoonfuls of mixture onto waxed paper
- You must work quickly or mixture will set up
- Once completely cooled, peel cookies off wax paper and store in air tight container

Let the words of my mouth, and the meditation of my heart, be acceptable in thy sight, O LORD, my strength, and my redeemer.
Psalms 19:14

Chocolate Chip Cookies

Ingredients:

2 1/4 cups All purpose flour
1 teaspoon Baking soda
1 teaspoon Salt
1 cup Softened butter
3/4 cup Granulated white sugar
3/4 cup packed brown sugar
2 Eggs
3 cups Semi-sweet chocolate chips
1 teaspoon Vanilla

And he said unto me, My grace is sufficient for thee: for my strength is made perfect in weakness. Most gladly therefore will I rather glory in my infirmities, that the power of Christ may rest upon me. - 2 Corinthians 12:9

- Combine flour, baking soda and salt
- In a large bowl, cream butter and sugar with mixer or by hand
- Add eggs and vanilla to butter and sugar, mix until combined
- Add flour mixture and mix until well combined
- Stir in chocolate chips until evenly distributed
- Refrigerate dough for at least 1 hour before baking
- Dough may be stored in the refrigerator for up to 2 weeks
- Use cookie scooper or large spoon to form dough into 1 to 1 ½ inch balls, this may be done before or after dough is placed in the refrigerator
- Place balls of dough on cookie sheet approximately 2 inches apart and bake 350° oven for approximately 8 minutes or until golden brown

I can do all things through Christ which strengtheneth me.
Philippians 4:13

Christmas Cookies

⁸And there were in the same country shepherds abiding in the field, keeping watch over their flock by night. ⁹And, lo, the angel of the Lord came upon them, and the glory of the Lord shone round about them: and they were sore afraid. ¹⁰And the angel said unto them, Fear not: for, behold, I bring you good tidings of great joy, which shall be to all people. **¹¹For unto you is born this day in the city of David a Saviour, which is Christ the Lord.** ¹²And this SHALL BE a sign unto you; Ye shall find the babe wrapped in swaddling clothes, lying in a manger. ¹³And suddenly there was with the angel a multitude of the heavenly host praising God, and saying, ¹⁴Glory to God in the highest, and on earth peace, good will toward men. - Luke 2

Ingredients:

4 cups All purpose flour
2 teaspoons Baking soda
1/2 teaspoon Salt
1 1/2 cup Sugar
1 1/2 cup Real butter
1/2 cup Heavy cream
2 Eggs
1 to 2 teaspoons Real vanilla

Butter cream frosting
Page 90
Food coloring

- Combine flour, baking soda and salt
- Using a mixer to cream butter and sugar until fluffy and smooth
- Add eggs, cream and vanilla, mix until well combined
- Add flour mixture and mix until smooth and creamy
- Place dough in refrigerator for at least 1 hour
- Roll out onto floured surface to approximately ¼ inch and cut into desired shapes
- Place on cookie sheet approximately 2 inches apart and bake in 350° oven for 8 to 10 minutes until golden brown
- Colored sugar may be sprinkled on cookies before baking
- Let cool at least 1 minute before removing from pan
- Let cool completely before decorating with colored frosting
- Dough may be stored in refrigerator for up to 2 weeks before baking

Oatmeal Raisin Cookies

15Beware of false prophets, which come to you in sheep's clothing, but inwardly they are ravening wolves. 16 Ye shall know them by their fruits. Do men gather grapes of thorns, or figs of thistles? 17 Even so every good tree bringeth forth good fruit; but a corrupt tree bringeth forth evil fruit. 18 A good tree cannot bring forth evil fruit, neither can a corrupt tree bring forth good fruit. 19 Every tree that bringeth not forth good fruit is hewn down, and cast into the fire. 20 Wherefore by their fruits ye shall know them.

Matthew 7

Ingredients:

3/4 cup Brown sugar
3/4 cup Regular sugar
1/2 cup Real butter
1/2 cup Applesauce
2 Eggs
2 teaspoons Real vanilla extract
2 cups All purpose flour
2 teaspoons Baking soda
1 tablespoon Cinnamon
3 1/4 cups Oats
2 1/2 cups Raisins
1/2 cup Ground flax seed

- Combine flour, flax seed, cinnamon, baking soda and salt
- In a large bowl, cream butter and sugar with mixer or by hand
- Add eggs, apple sauce and vanilla to butter and sugar mix until combined
- Add flour mixture and mix until well combined
- Stir in oatmeal and raisins until evenly distributed
- Refrigerate dough for at least 1 hour before baking
- Dough may be stored in the refrigerator for up to 2 weeks
- Use cookie scooper or large spoon to form dough into 1 to 1 ½ inch balls, this may be done before or after dough is placed in the refrigerator
- Place balls of dough on cookie sheet approximately 2 inches apart and bake 350° oven for approximately 8 minutes or until golden brown

Blessed be the God and Father of our Lord Jesus Christ, which according to his abundant mercy hath begotten us again unto a lively hope by the resurrection of Jesus Christ from the dead.
1 Peter 1:3

Cranberry Orange Scones

For his anger endureth but a moment;
in his favour is life:
weeping may endure for a night,
but joy cometh in the morning.
Psalm 30:5

Ingredients:

2 1/2 cups all
purpose flour
3/4 cup sugar
1/2 cup butter,
softened
1/2 cup sour cream
1/4 cup honey
2 eggs
2 teaspoons freshly
grated orange peel
1 teaspoon vanilla
1/2 teaspoon
baking soda 1/2
teaspoon salt
1 cup sweetened
dried cranberries

Glaze
1 1/2 cups
powdered sugar
1 tablespoon
butter, softened 1
to 3 tablespoons
orange juice

- Zest orange and combine with all dry ingredients
- Add all wet ingredients to mixture and mix until creamy and well combined
- Fold in cranberries
- Scoop cookie dough onto greased cookie sheet and bake in preheated 350° oven for 12 to 14 minutes or until golden brown
- While cookies are baking combine ingredients for glaze and add only enough orange juice to make glaze pourable
- Let cookies cool on pan for 3 or 4 minutes
- Remove cookies from pan and glaze while still warm

Recipe and photos by
Samantha Mullins

Ye have not chosen me, but I have chosen you, and ordained you, that ye should go and bring forth fruit, and that your fruit should remain: that whatsoever ye shall ask of the Father in my name, he may give it you. - John 15:16

Set a watch, O LORD, before my mouth; keep the door of my lips.
Psalms 141:3

Apple Cobbler

Ingredients:

At least 9 cups of sliced apples (7 to 10 apples)
3/4 cup sugar
1 teaspoon cinnamon
2 cups all purpose flour
2 cups sugar
2 eggs
3 teaspoons baking powder
3/4 teaspoon salt
1 1/2 sticks butter (3/4 cup)

- Put apples in baking pan
- Combine sugar & cinnamon and mix in apples, coating the apples
- Lightly beat eggs and add to flour, baking powder and salt mixture, mix until well combined and crumbly
- Dump flour mixture over apples
- Pour melted butter over top of other ingredients
- Do not mix any ingredients once they have been added to the pan
- Bake in preheated 350° oven for 45 to 60 minutes, until golden brown and bubbling
- Best served hot with ice cream on top

[30] And thou shalt love the Lord thy God with all thy heart, and with all thy soul, and with all thy mind, and with all thy strength: this is the first commandment.

[31] And the second is like, namely this, Thou shalt love thy neighbour as thyself. There is none other commandment greater than these.

Mark 12

Blackberry Cobbler

Ingredients:

4 cups
Blackberries
1 cup Sugar
1 cup All purpose
flour
1 Egg
1 teaspoon Real
vanilla extract
1/2 cup Real
butter

- Butter casserole dish and pour berries in. Sprinkle with vanilla
- In a bowl, beat eggs, add flour and sugar mix until crumbly, spread mixture over berries
- Pour melted butter over top of cobbler and sprinkle top with one tablespoon of sugar
- Bake in preheated 375° oven for 35 minutes or until brown and bubbly

And not only so, but we glory in tribulations also: knowing that tribulation worketh patience; And patience, experience; and experience, hope.
Romans 5:3-4

Peach Cobbler

Ingredients:

1/2 cup butter
1 cup all purpose flour
1 1/2 cups sugar
1 tablespoon baking powder
1/4 teaspoon salt
1 cup milk
4 or more cups peaches
1 tablespoon lemon juice

- In pot on medium heat, combine peaches, lemon juice and 1 cup of sugar bring to a boil
- Melt butter in baking pan
- Combine flour, 1 cup of sugar, baking powder, salt and milk
- Pour flour mixture into melted butter, do not stir
- Pour peach mixture over flour mixture and butter, do not stir
- Bake in preheated 375° oven for 40 to 45 minutes, until golden brown and bubbling

And the fruit of righteousness is sown in peace of them that make peace. - James 3:18

Blueberry Buckle

Ingredients:

3/4 cup sugar
1/4 cup butter
1 egg
1 1/2 cups AP flour
1 tablespoon baking
Powder
1 tablespoon flour
1 1/2 to 2 1/2 cups blueberries
1/2 teaspoon salt
1/2 cup milk

Topping:
4 tablespoons butter
1/2 cup sugar
1/3 cup AP flour
1/2 teaspoon cinnamon

For God hath not given us the spirit of fear; but of power,
and of love, and of a sound mind. - 2 Timothy 1:7

- Combine blueberries and 1 tablespoon of flour and toss until blueberries are coated
- Combine sugar, butter and egg cream until fluffy
- Combine flour, baking powder and salt
- Add flour mixture and milk to creamed sugar and butter, mix until combined
- Fold in blueberries
- Pour batter into greased 8 x 8 oven safe pan
- Combine topping ingredients and mix with fork or pastry blade until crumbly. Do not over mix. Topping should be crumbly and not creamed
- Sprinkle topping evenly over top of batter
- Bake in a preheated 350° oven for 40 to 45 minutes

Apple Dumplings

Ingredients:

2 pie crusts
6 apples
1/2 cup of butter
3/4 cup of brown sugar
1 teaspoon of cinnamon
1/2 teaspoon of nutmeg
2 cups of water
2 cups of sugar
1 teaspoon of real vanilla

If ye walk in my statutes, and keep my commandments, and do them; Then I will give you rain in due season, and the land shall yield her increase, and the trees of the field shall yield their fruit.

Leviticus 26:3-4

- Divide pie crust dough into 6 equal portions and roll into a square large enough to cover 1 apple
- Combine brown sugar, cinnamon and nutmeg
- Peel and core apples leaving the apple intact, an apple corer makes this task easier
- Place each apple on dough square
- Equally divide brown sugar and spices, filling the center of each apple with mixture
- Cut butter in 6 equal pieces and place on top of each apple
- Pull crust up around apple and seal edges firmly
- Place sealed apples in baking dish making sure sides are not touching
- In pot on stove, bring water, sugar and vanilla to a boil stirring occasionally, continue to boil for 3 to 5 minutes until mixture thickens slightly
- Pour syrup mixture over dumplings
- Bake in preheated 400° oven for 45 to 60 minutes, until golden brown and apples are tender

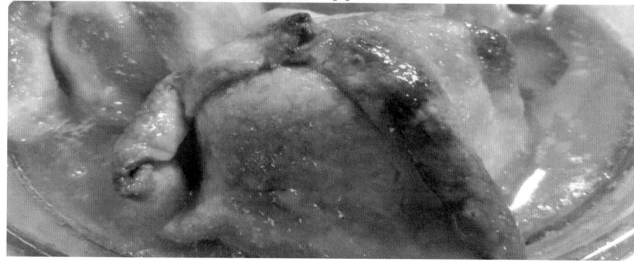

Pie Crust

Ingredients for double crust:

3 cups - All purpose flour
1 teaspoon - Salt
1 cup - Butter
½ to 2/3 cup- Ice water

[14] Ye are the light of the world. A city that is set on an hill cannot be hid. [15] Neither do men light a candle, and put it under a bushel, but on a candlestick; and it giveth light unto all that are in the house. [16] Let your light so shine before men, that they may see your good works, and glorify your Father which is in heaven.

Matthew 5

- **Combine flour and salt**
- **Cut butter in with fork, pastry blade or food processer**
- **Add water 1 tablespoon at a time as you mix until mixture is crumbly but will stick together**
- **Squeeze mixture into ball, wrap tightly and place in refrigerator for at least 1 hour**
- **Divide dough into 2 equal portions and roll out on well floured surface**
- **Place in pie pan**
- **For pies that require prebaked crust, poke several holes In crust with fork**
- **Bake in preheated 350° oven for approximately 30 minutes or until golden brown**
- **Cool completely before filling**

[24] For there shall arise false Christs, and false prophets, and shall shew great signs and wonders; insomuch that, if it were possible, they shall deceive the very elect.[25] Behold, I have told you before.[26] Wherefore if they shall say unto you, Behold, he is in the desert; go not forth: behold, he is in the secret chambers; believe it not.[27] For as the lightning cometh out of the east, and shineth even unto the west; so shall also the coming of the Son of man be.[28] For wheresoever the carcase is, there will the eagles be gathered together.[29] Immediately after the tribulation of those days shall the sun be darkened, and the moon shall not give her light, and the stars shall fall from heaven, and the powers of the heavens shall be shaken:[30] And then shall appear the sign of the Son of man in heaven: and then shall all the tribes of the earth mourn, and they shall see the Son of man coming in the clouds of heaven with power and great glory.[31] And he shall send his angels with a great sound of a trumpet, and they shall gather together his elect from the four winds, from one end of heaven to the other. – Matthew 24

Crumb Pie Crust

Ingredients:

1 1/2 cups crumbs
(about 6 oz.)
1/4 cup sugar
(optional)
6 tablespoons
melted butter

- Crust may be made with graham crackers, chocolate graham crackers, vanilla wafers or any other crisp cookie
- Crush cookies into fine crumbs by placing in plastic bag and pounding or put in a food processor
- Combine crumbs, sugar and butter
- Press crumbs into pie pan and place in refrigerator 1 hour before filling

12 Then spake Jesus again unto them, saying, I am the light of the world: he that followeth me shall not walk in darkness, but shall have the light of life. – John 8

Pecan Pie

Ingredients:

Unbaked 9 inch
pie shell
1 cup white corn
syrup
1/2 cup Brown
sugar packed
1/4 teaspoon Salt
1 teaspoon
vanilla
2 teaspoons
Lemon juice
3 Eggs
1 cup Pecans

- In a large bowl, beat eggs
- Add all other ingredients and mix until well combined
- Pour ingredients into prepared unbaked pie shell
- Bake in a preheated 400° oven for 10 minutes then reduce heat to 350° and continue to bake for 50 to 60 minutes
- To prevent burning, pie may be tented with heavy duty foil for the first 30 minutes of baking

Apple Pie

Ingredients:

6 to 8 cups peeled and sliced apples of choice
1 tablespoon vinegar or lemon juice
2 to 4 tablespoons real butter
1/4 cup flour
1/2 to 1 cups sugar
1 teaspoon cinnamon
1/2 teaspoon salt
1/3 teaspoon ginger
1/3 teaspoon nutmeg
1/3 teaspoon allspice

2 pie crusts
1 egg white
1 teaspoon sugar
pinch of cinnamon

For he that will love life, and see good days, let him refrain his
tongue from evil, and his lips that they speak no guile:
1 Peter 3:10

- In a large bowl combine apples, vinegar and vanilla
- Combine flour, sugar and spices
- Add spice mixture to apples and toss until well combined
- Line pie plate with crust
- Pour apple mixture into pie crust
- Top apples with slices of butter
- Cover apples with pie crust and seal edges of crust together
- Whip egg white until slightly foamy and brush on top of crust making sure to coat entire crust
- Sprinkle top crust with sugar and cinnamon
- Cut large X in center of pie crust and several X's around top crust to allow pie to vent during baking
- Bake in a preheated 425° oven for 15 minutes, reduce heat to 375° and continue to bake for 45 to 50 minutes
- To prevent pie from burning on top, it may be tented with heavy duty foil for the first 30 minutes of baking

[31] What shall we then say to these things? If God be for us, who can be against us? [32] He that spared not his own Son, but delivered him up for us all, how shall he not with him also freely give us all things? [33] Who shall lay any thing to the charge of God's elect? It is God that justifieth. [34] Who is he that condemneth? It is Christ that died, yea rather, that is risen again, who is even at the right hand of God, who also maketh intercession for us. – Romans 8

Buttermilk Pie

Ingredients:

1 to 2 cups Sugar
(You decide how
sweet you want it)
1/2 cup melted
butter
3 tablespoons All
purpose flour
3 Eggs
1/4 teaspoon Salt
1 teaspoon Vanilla
extract
1 cup Buttermilk
9 inch unbaked
pie crust

- In a large bowl, beat eggs
- Add all other ingredients and mix until well combined
- Pour ingredients into prepared unbaked pie crust
- Bake in a preheated 400° oven for 10 minutes then reduce heat to 350° and continue to bake for 50 to 60 minutes
- To prevent burning, pie may be tented with heavy duty foil for the first 30 minutes of baking

Cherry Pie Filling

Ingredients:

5 to 6 cups fresh pitted cherries
1 cup water
1/4 cup corn starch
2 tablespoons lemon juice (optional)
1/2 to 1 cup sugar

- Dissolve water in cornstarch
- Combine all ingredients in pot
- Cook on medium heat, stirring constantly until mixture is thick and not cloudy

I use this for all my desserts that call for cherry pie filling because all of the commercial pie fillings have high fructose corn syrup and if I am going to the trouble to make homemade desserts I don't want that stuff in them.

A soft answer turneth away wrath: but grievous words stir up anger. Proverbs 15:1

Pumpkin Pie

But let him ask in faith, nothing wavering. For he that wavereth is like a wave of the sea driven with the wind and tossed. - James 1:6

Ingredients:

15 ounce can pumpkin
12 ounce can Evaporated milk
2 Eggs
3/4 cup Packed brown sugar
1/2 teaspoon Salt
1 teaspoon Cinnamon
1/2 teaspoon Ginger
1/4 teaspoon Nutmeg
1/4 teaspoon Cloves
Unbaked 9 inch pie crust

- In a large bowl, beat eggs
- Combine sugar, flour and spices for easier mixing
- Combine all ingredients and mix until well combined
- Pour ingredients into prepared, unbaked pie crust
- Bake in a preheated 425° oven for 10 minutes then reduce heat to 350° and continue to bake for 40 to 50 minutes
- To prevent burning, pie may be tented with heavy duty foil for the first 30 minutes of baking

[4] You are of God, little children, and have overcome them, because He who is in you is greater than he who is in the world. [5] They are of the world. Therefore they speak *as* of the world, and the world hears them. [6] We are of God. He who knows God hears us; he who is not of God does not hear us. By this we know the spirit of truth and the spirit of error. – 1 John 4

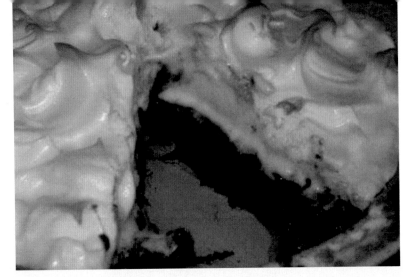

Chocolate Cream Pie

Ingredients:

2 cups Milk
1/4 cup Corn starch
1/3 cup Cocoa
1 1/2 cup Sugar
2 tablespoons Butter
3 Egg yolks
1 teaspoon Vanilla
1 Baked pie crust

- In a pot, combine milk, corn starch, cocoa, sugar, egg yolks, butter and cook over medium heat, stirring constantly until mixture thickens
- Once mixture has come to a boil and started to thicken, add vanilla and mix until combined
- Pour hot mixture into baked pie shell; if you are topping with meringue, add your meringue while filling is hot.
- Refrigerate at least 6 hours or overnight

Death and life [are] in the power of the tongue: and they that love it shall eat the fruit thereof. - Proverbs 18:21

Meringue

Ingredients:

3 Egg whites
1/4 cup Sugar
1/2 teaspoon Real
vanilla extract
(¼ teaspoon of
cream of tartar or
1teaspoon of
lemon juice can
be added to help
stabilize
meringue)

- Beat egg whites until stiff peaks form
- Continue to beat while slowly adding remaining ingredients
- Carefully add to the top of hot pie or other dessert
- Bake in a pre-heated 425° oven for 4 or 5 minutes until golden brown
- Meringue is a light, fluffy, old fashioned topping for pies, puddings, cookies and cakes.

And he said, The things which are impossible with men are possible with God. - Luke 18:27

Chocolate Pudding Pie

Ingredients:

8 Ounces of milk
chocolate
1 tablespoon of real
vanilla extract
2 tablespoons of
real butter
4 egg yolks
3 cups of milk
1/4 teaspoon of salt
2 tablespoons of
unsweetened
cocoa
6 tablespoons of
corn starch
2/3 cup of sugar
Chocolate crumb
crust

- Combine sugar, cocoa, cornstarch and salt in pan
- Combine egg yolks and milk in bowl and mix
- Stir egg yolks into sugar mixture
- Cook over medium heat, stirring constantly until mixture comes to a boil
- Continue to cook and stir for approximately 1 minute, mixture will thicken
- Remove from heat, stir in butter and vanilla
- Pour mixture into prepared crust
- Cover with plastic wrap and place pie in refrigerator for several hours until completely cool
- Serve with whipped cream if desired

Creamy Lemon Pie

Ingredients:
1/2 cup fresh squeezed lemon juice
1 to 2 tablespoons fresh lemon zest
14 ounce can sweetened condensed milk
8 ounces softened cream cheese
Vanilla wafer crumb crust (page 116)

- Combine all ingredients and mix until smooth and well creamed
- Pour into prepared crust and refrigerate for at least 2 hours or place in freezer for approximately 30 minutes
- Add toppings when ready to serve
- Topping options: whipped cream, fresh blueberries, fresh raspberries or fresh strawberries.

Greater love hath no man than this, that a man lay down his life for his friends. John 15:13

Whipped Cream

Ingredients:

8 ounces
whipping cream
2 tablespoons
sugar
1/4 teaspoon
vanilla extract

- Chill bowl and beaters for best results
- Add whipping cream to chilled bowl and whip until firm
- Add sugar and vanilla while beating
- If ingredients become warm whipped cream will be runny

The Lord is not slack concerning his promise, as some men count slackness; but is longsuffering to us-ward, not willing that any should perish, but that all should come to repentance.
2 Peter 3:9

To every thing there is a season, and a time to every purpose under the heaven: - **Ecclesiastes 3:1**

Easy Summer Cake

Ingredients:

Sponge cake/Angel food cake
1 lb. Strawberries
1 lb. Bananas
1/3 to 1/2 cup sugar
Whipped cream

- Slice strawberries and bananas
- Add sugar to fruit and refrigerate for a few hours
- Cake may be sliced into two layers or individual pieces
- Top sliced cake with fruit mixture and whipped cream
- Serve as soon as possible

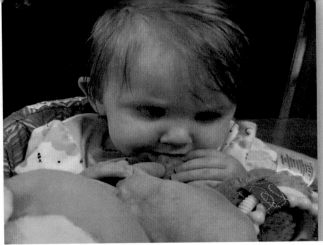

Teething Cookies

Ingredients:

1 cup All purpose flour
1 cup Baby rice cereal
1 Banana
2 teaspoons Cinnamon
2 tablespoons Oil
3 tablespoons Water

- Mash banana and mix all ingredients well
- Roll out on lightly flowered surface and cut into shapes
- Place on parchment lined cookie sheet
- Bake in a pre-heated 425° oven for 11 to 15 minutes until hard

Behold, children are a gift of the LORD,
The fruit of the womb is a reward.
Psalms 127:3

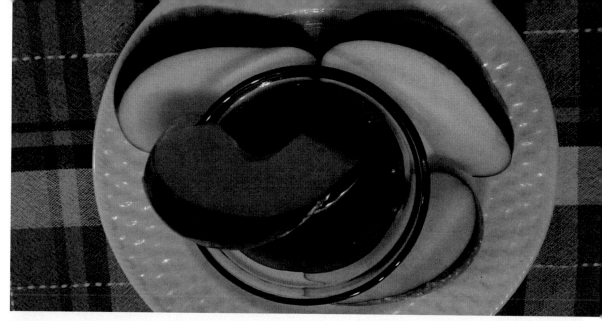

Caramel Sauce

Ingredients:

1/2 cup Real
unsalted butter
1/2 cup Packed
brown sugar
1/2 cup Heavy
cream
1 teaspoon Real
vanilla extract

- In a pot combine butter, brown sugar and cream
- Cook over medium heat, stirring constantly, bring to a boil and continue to cook and stir for 5 minutes
- Remove from heat and cool 5 minutes, stir in vanilla

Whom having not seen, ye love; in whom, though now ye see him not,
yet believing, ye rejoice with joy unspeakable and full of glory:
Receiving the end of your faith, even the salvation of your souls.
1 Peter 1:8-9

Chocolate Syrup

Ingredients:

1 cup Water
1 1/2 cup Sugar
1 cup Cocoa
1/8 teaspoon Salt
1 teaspoon Real vanilla

- In a pot, combine sugar, cocoa and salt
- Add water
- Cook over medium heat, stirring constantly, bring to a boil, continue to cook and stir for 3 minutes
- Remove from heat and stir in vanilla

But as it is written, Eye hath not seen, nor ear heard, neither have entered into the heart of man, the things which God hath prepared for them that love him.
1 Corinthians 2:9

Chocolate Fudge

Ingredients:

3 cups Sugar
3/4 cups Real butter
3/4 cups Evaporated milk
12 ounces Semi - sweet chocolate
1 teaspoon Vanilla
7 ounce jar marshmallow cream
Optional **
1 cup - Chopped walnuts

- In a large pot, combine sugar, butter and milk
- Over medium heat, stir constantly, bring to a boil and continue to cook and stir 5 minutes or until you reach 234° on candy thermometer
- Remove from heat, working very quickly, stir in chocolate, vanilla and marshmallow cream
- Stir vigorously until very well combined and creamy
- While mixture is still hot, pour onto greased or lined cookie sheet
- Allow to cool and cut into 1" squares

Peanut Butter Fudge

Ingredients:

1 1/2 cups Jif
Peanut butter
Seven ounce jar
Jet-Puffed
marshmallow
cream
3/4 cup
Evaporated milk
3 cups Sugar
6 tablespoons
Real butter
1 teaspoon Real
vanilla

- In a large pot, combine sugar, butter and milk
- Over medium heat, stir constantly, bring to a boil and continue to cook and stir 5 minutes or until you reach 234° on candy thermometer
- Remove from heat, working very quickly, stir in peanut butter, vanilla and marshmallow cream
- Stir vigorously until very well combined and creamy
- While mixture is still hot, pour onto greased or lined cookie sheet
- Allow to cool and cut into 1" squares

Chocolate Nut Clusters

Ingredients:

1/2 cup - Milk chocolate chips
1/2 cup - Semi - sweet chocolate chips
1 tablespoon - Coconut oil
1/2 cup - Peanuts
1/2 cup - Cashews

- Melt chocolate and coconut oil in microwave, crock pot or in pot on stove using very low heat
- Stir in nuts
- Scoop tablespoon of mixture and drop onto waxed paper
- Allow to completely cool, remove from paper and store in air tight container
- Any kind of nuts may be substituted

Therefore I say unto you, What things soever ye desire, when ye pray, believe that ye receive them, and ye shall have them. Mark 11:24

Divinity

Put the 1 cup sugar, ½ cup water and cream of tartar into saucepan; stir to blend, and then boil rapidly without stirring to 240° F or until syrup will spin a thread 6 inches long when dropped from a metal spoon. Immediately remove from heat. Meanwhile, beat egg whites until stiff. In another saucepan, I have combined the 2 cups sugar, corn syrup, salt and ¼ cup water. When the first mixture is done, place the second mixture over the heat and boil with occasional stirring until syrup reaches 280° F. (medium crack stage). Meanwhile, pour the first syrup while hot over egg whites, adding slowly and beating continuously until stiff and smooth. Set aside until second syrup is done. Cool a minute or two, then pour it slowly over first mixture, continuing to beat until smooth and so stiff that it is hard to mix. Add flavoring and nuts, then turn into buttered pan, and press out smooth. When Divinity is set, cut into squares. This recipe makes about 2 pounds.

Ingredients:

Pot #1
1 cup Sugar
1/2 cup Water
1/8 teaspoon Cream of tartar
Pot #2
2 cups Sugar
2/3 cup White corn syrup
1/4 teaspoon Salt
1/4 cup Water
Uncooked Ingredients:
3 Egg whites
1 teaspoon Real vanilla
1 cup Finely chopped nuts. (I used pecans)
Candied fruits, such as cherries and pineapple may be cut fine and folded in before candy cools for attractive color.

Peanut Butter Pinwheels

Ingredients:

2 1/2 cups
Granulated sugar
1/2 cup White corn
syrup
1/2 cup Water
3 Egg whites
4 lbs. Powdered
sugar (You won't
use all of it)
1 1/2 - 18 oz. Jars
of peanut butter

- In a pot, combine sugar, corn syrup and water and heat over medium heat until syrup thickens and forms threads
- While syrup is cooking, beat egg whites until fluffy and stiff
- While mixing add ½ of syrup to egg whites then add 1 cup of powdered sugar then add other ½ of syrup then continue to add powdered sugar a little at a time until dough consistency is reached. Do not stop mixing during this process
- Turn dough out onto surface that is well coated with powdered sugar

For where two or three are gathered together in my name, there am I in the midst of them.
Matthew 18:20

- **Knead dough adding powdered sugar as needed until it is no longer sticky. Work quickly; if dough cools it will become crumbly and hard to work with.**
- **Roll out to approximately ¼ inch thick and spread with peanut butter**
- **Roll up into rolls and wrap tightly in plastic wrap**
- **Place in refrigerator until cool and firm**
- **Once cooled, slice candy to desired thickness and store in air tight container**

Peanut Butter Cups

Ingredients for filling:

1 cup Peanut butter

1 1/3 cups Powdered sugar

4 tablespoons Softened real butter

1 teaspoon Real vanilla

Ingredients for the chocolate dip:

1 cup Semi - sweet chocolate chips

1 cup Milk chocolate chips

2 tablespoons Coconut oil or shortening -or-

2 cups - Dark melting wafers for candy making and dipping

Ingredients for the drizzle:

1/2 cup White baking pieces

1/2 tablespoon Coconut oil or shortening

Call unto me, and I will answer thee, and show thee great and mighty things, which thou knowest not. - Jeremiah 33:3

- Combine filling ingredients in bowl and cream
- Scoop or spoon filling onto wax paper lined baking sheet, forming into 1 inch balls
- Refrigerate until firm
- Melt chocolate and coconut oil in microwave or crock pot
- Dip peanut butter balls on chocolate and place on line cookie sheet or in candy cups
- Drizzle with melted white chocolate and coconut oil mixture to decorate if desired

Enter ye in at the strait gate: for wide is the gate, and broad is the way, that leadeth to destruction, and many there be which go in thereat: Because strait is the gate, and narrow is the way, which leadeth unto life, and few there be that find it.
Matthew 7:13-14

Martha Washington Candy

The Lord is nigh unto all them that call upon him,
to all that call upon him in truth. - Psalm 145:18

For I am not ashamed of the gospel of Christ: for it is the power of God unto salvation to every one that believeth; to the Jew first, and also to the Greek. - Romans 1:16

Ingredients:

3 cups sweetened coconut
14 ounces sweetened condensed milk
4 cups powdered sugar
1 cup real butter
2 cups chopped pecans
1 to 2 teaspoons real vanilla extract

Dip Ingredients

1 cup semi-sweet chocolate chips
1 cup milk chocolate chips
2 tablespoons coconut oil

- Combine all candy ingredients in a large bowl and mix until well combined
- Form into 1 inch balls and place on wax paper lined baking sheet
- Chill for at least 1 hour
- Combine dip ingredients in a small bowl and melt in microwave, crock pot or in pot on stove on very low heat
- Dip candy balls into melted chocolate making sure to completely coat and return to wax paper to cool
- Dip may be reheated if it cools and becomes too stiff while working
- Add sprinkles, flaked coconut, chopped nuts or other decorative touches while chocolate coating is warm and soft if desired
- Once candy is cooled and chocolate coating is firm, store in air tight container in refrigerator

Chocolate Cherry Bombs

Ingredients:

Leftover cake
crumbs
Leftover frosting
White baking
pieces
Dark chocolate
candy coating
pieces
Maraschino
cherries with
stems attached
1 tablespoon
coconut oil per cup
of dip

- Combine cake crumbs and frosting until consistency is pasty
- Drain cherries and dry on paper towel
- Wrap crumb mixture around cherries and place on wax paper lined baking sheet
- Refrigerate until firm
- Combine dip ingredients and melt
- Dip cherry cake balls and return to wax paper or candy cups, decorate if desired
- Store in air tight container in refrigerator

Chocolate Truffles

Ingredients:

1 cup Whipping cream
1/4 cup Packed brown sugar
1/4 teaspoon Salt
1 teaspoon Real vanilla
12 oz. Semi sweet chocolate
12 oz. Milk chocolate

- In pot on medium low heat, combine all ingredients, stirring constantly, until chocolate is melted and mixture is creamy
- Remove from heat and pour mixture into shallow pan
- Refrigerate until mixture is firm
- Scoop mixture out with cookie scoop or spoon and form into 1 inch balls
- Place candy balls onto wax paper lined baking sheet and return to refrigerator until firm
- Once firm cover by rolling in chopped nuts, peppermint, dark chocolate or by dipping in melted chocolate(see page 143)
- Store candy in air tight container in refrigerator

Vanilla Ice Cream

Ingredients:

1/2 gallon Half and half
1 1/2 cups Sugar
2 teaspoons Real vanilla extract

- **Combine ingredients and add to ice cream maker**
- **Churn until ice cream starts to stiffen**
- **Place in freezer for about two hours to set very firm**

[14] Now therefore fear the LORD, and serve him in sincerity and in truth: and put away the gods which your fathers served on the other side of the flood, and in Egypt; and serve ye the LORD. [15] And if it seem evil unto you to serve the LORD, choose you this day whom ye will serve; whether the gods which your fathers served that were on the other side of the flood, or the gods of the Amorites, in whose land ye dwell: but as for me and my house, we will serve the LORD.

Joshua 24:14-15

Strawberry Mousse

Ingredients:

2 cups Strawberries
1 pack Gelatin
1/3 cup Water
3/4 cup Sugar
1 tablespoon Lemon juice
2 cups Heavy cream

Recipe and photo by Samantha Mullins

- Purée strawberries in blender or food processor and add sugar and lemon juice and return to blender
- Slowly combine gelatin and water, reserving the last 2 tablespoons of water and heat in microwave until very hot, then add to gelatin after 2 minutes
- Combine gelatin and strawberries
- Whip the cream until stiff and carefully fold in strawberry mixture
- Refrigerate until stiff

But Jesus said, Suffer little children, and forbid them not, to come unto me: for of such is the kingdom of heaven.
Matthew 19:14

Strawberries and Cream

Ingredients:

A pint of fresh strawberries
1 tablespoon of sugar (optional)

Whipped cream

- **Wash berries and slice**
- **Place in large bowl and sprinkle with sugar**
- **Place in fridge for an hour to a few days**
- **Whip cream page 126**
- **Divide berries in cups and top with whipped cream when ready to serve**

[13] Happy [is] the man [that] findeth wisdom, and the man [that] getteth understanding. [14] For the merchandise of it [is] better than the merchandise of silver, and the gain thereof than fine gold. [15] She [is] more precious than rubies: and all the things thou canst desire are not to be compared unto her. [16] Length of days [is] in her right hand; [and] in her left hand riches and honour. [17] Her ways [are] ways of pleasantness, and all her paths [are] peace. [18] She [is] a tree of life to them that lay hold upon her: and happy [is every one] that retaineth her. – **Proverbs 3**

Cream Cheese Fruit Dip

Ingredients:

8 oz. cream cheese
7 or 8 oz. marshmallow cream
Fresh fruit

- Soften cream cheese to room temperature
- Mix cream cheese and marshmallow cream together until smooth
- Wash fruit well
- Can be used to dip almost any fruit or put in piping bag and used to stuff fruit

But the fruit of the Spirit is love, joy, peace, longsuffering, gentleness, goodness, faith, Meekness, temperance: against such there is no law. - Galatians 5:22-23

Lemonade

Ingredients:

5 to 8 fresh lemons, depending on their size
(1 ½ to 2 cups lemon juice)
1 to 1 1/2 cups of sugar Filtered Water

- Wash lemons, zest and juice
- Combine lemon juice, zest, sugar and enough water to equal ½ gallon
- Mix until well combined and sugar is dissolved
- Chill and serve over ice

But whosoever drinketh of the water that I shall give him shall never thirst; but the water that I shall give him shall be in him a well of water springing up into everlasting life. - John 4:14

Sweet Tea

Ingredients:

2 family sized
tea bags
½ to 1 cup sugar
Filtered water
Ice

- Brew tea in coffee pot or by steeping in hot water or place tea bags in water and set in the sun for an hour or two
- Add sugar to warm tea and stir until dissolved
- Fill a glass with ice and pour tea over ice
- Have a seat in a porch rocker and enjoy life

I will greatly rejoice in the Lord, my soul shall be joyful in my God; for he hath clothed me with the garments of salvation, he hath covered me with the robe of righteousness, as a bridegroom decketh himself with ornaments, and as a bride adorneth herself with her jewels. - Isaiah 61:10

Snow Cream

Ingredients:

A big bowl of fresh clean snow

Milk

Sugar

Vanilla

Kids (of any age)

- Whisk sugar, milk and vanilla into snow, adding a little at a time to adjust consistency and taste
- Enjoy under a blanked while you watch a movie and create some warm memories

This recipe started the Hillbilly kitchen so I thought it was fittin' to make it the last recipe in the book. Some of my best childhood memories are of days when we had snow cream and some of my favorite memories of my children are from those snow days that we always ended with a big bowl of snow cream and a movie.

This is my commandment, That ye love one another, as I have loved you. - John 15:12

The people I come from:

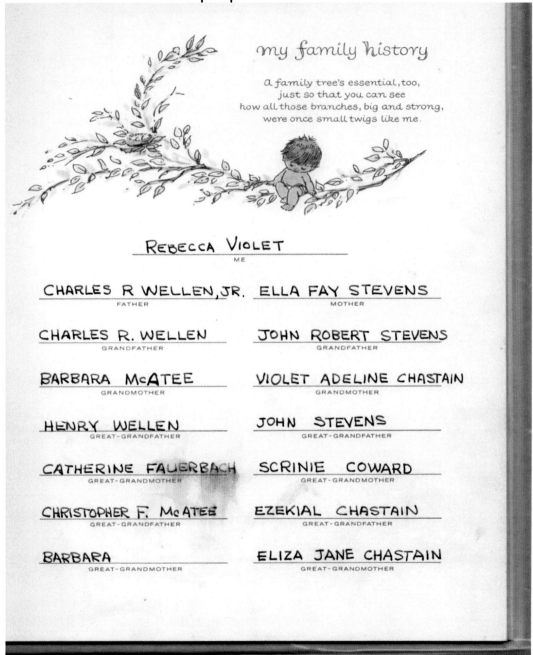

my family history

A family tree's essential, too,
just so that you can see
how all those branches, big and strong,
were once small twigs like me.

REBECCA VIOLET
ME

CHARLES R WELLEN, JR.
FATHER

ELLA FAY STEVENS
MOTHER

CHARLES R. WELLEN
GRANDFATHER

JOHN ROBERT STEVENS
GRANDFATHER

BARBARA McATEE
GRANDMOTHER

VIOLET ADELINE CHASTAIN
GRANDMOTHER

HENRY WELLEN
GREAT-GRANDFATHER

JOHN STEVENS
GREAT-GRANDFATHER

CATHERINE FAUERBACH
GREAT-GRANDMOTHER

SCRINIE COWARD
GREAT-GRANDMOTHER

CHRISTOPHER F. McATEE
GREAT-GRANDFATHER

EZEKIAL CHASTAIN
GREAT-GRANDFATHER

BARBARA
GREAT-GRANDMOTHER

ELIZA JANE CHASTAIN
GREAT-GRANDMOTHER

You know more about yourself, if you know where you came from.
A strange personal observation: My mom's last name was Stephens. My
dad never misspells anything, but he misspelled my mom's maiden name!?!?

Staff photo by CLIFF McBRIDE

Charlie and Barbara Wellen, shown at their Seffner home with a photo from their youth, marked 71 years of marriage Thursday.

My Popop during World War II, in France (I think). He sent this to Nanny and his two young sons (my dad was the oldest)

Yours with all of my love

I wasn't as close to my dad's parents simply because they did not live close. However, the impact of my Nanny and Popop in my life would take a book to share properly. I never doubted their love. They expanded my world far beyond the mountain valley that I grew up in. Because of them, I knew what a big exciting place the world is and because of their example, I knew the world was a far better place with God and a lifelong partner.

Wellen family photos

Barbara and Charlie Wellen share 71 years of memories. From top right are photos of Barbara at high school graduation, a young Charlie and the couple in middle age.

"He's for me and I'm for him," Barbara says of her love for Charlie.

Barbara poses at home with three of their kids while Charlie was at war.

EVENT PREVIEW

Catholic Diocese of St. Petersburg Wedding Jubilee Mass

WHEN: 3 p.m. Feb. 28

WHERE: Cathedral of St. Jude the Apostle, 5815 Fifth Ave. N., St. Petersburg

CELEBRATES: Couples married 25 years, 50 years or more in 2010. Of the 383 couples registered, 53 will mark 25 years of marriage; 134 will hit 50; 75 celebrate more than 60 years. Charlie and Barbara Wellen are the longest wed at 71 year

my first Christmas

When first I saw a Christmas ball,
I saw reflected there
a million tiny, sparkling lights
and happiness everywhere.

1968

HISTORICAL NOTE: THREE AMERICANS LEFT A LUNAR ORBIT THIS MORNING AT ABOUT 1:30 FOR THEIR RETURN TO THE EARTH. THIS WAS MAN'S FIRST TRIP TO THE MOON.

MOMMY AND DADDY GOT ME A SWING. SANTA GAVE ME A BIG DOLL AND A PINK ELEPHANT. AUNT EFFIE GOT ME A SLEEPER. AUNT SUSIE SENT CLOTHES. GRANNIE STEVENS GAVE ME A DOLL. BUT THE BEST OF ALL IS MY PINK AND YELLOW TEDDY BEAR THAT GRANNY WELLEN SENT FROM FLORIDA.

PAW STEPHENS GAVE ME A BLUE DRESS AND PANTS.

my first birthday

When I arrived upon this earth,
I wasn't even one.
But today I had a birthday,
and say! did we have fun!

WE MOVED TO BLACK MOUNTAIN IN JULY AND
NOBODY KNOWS US TO COME TO MY BIRTHDAY.
PARTY. MOMMY AND DADDY ARE SAD, AND
ONE OLD LADY CAME. DADDY TOOK A COUPLE
OF PICTURES OF ME WITH CAKE ON MY
FACE, BUT DADDY IS NOT WORKING AND WE
ARE POOR.

Other birthdays

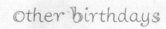

2 YRS OLD — DADDY IS OUT OF WORK MOMMY & DADDY GOT ME A DOLLY WHO IS BIGGER THAN ME. I NAMED HER "CANDY."

3 YRS OLD — A LOT HAPPENED TO ME IN THE LAST YEAR. TIMES HAVE BEEN HARD AND DADDY WAS GOING TO MOVE US TO ALBUQUERQUE, NEW MEXICO. MOMMY AND I WERE STAYING AT GRANNY'S, BECAUSE MOMMY WAS GOING TO HAVE A BABY. DADDY HAD A BAD ACCIDENT IN ARKANSAS AND BROKE HIS HIP. SO DADDY WAS NOT WORKING THIS YEAR, EITHER. I HAD A PARTY AT MANY FORKS CHURCH ON GUMLOG AND MOMMY & DADDY GOT ME A RED WAGON AND A BIG BAG OF BUILDING BLOCKS. I GOT A LOT OF OTHER STUFF, TOO.

4 YEARS OLD — WE ARE IN SYLVA, N.C. AND DADDY IS A COLLEGE STUDENT. MOMMY AND DADDY GOT ME MRS. BEASLEY, BRIAN & WENDY GAVE ME A DRESSER SET CHRISTY & MONTY GAVE ME PIGGY BANK MONEY, ZENA & THADDY GAVE ME A SWIMMING POOL. WE HAD A LEMON CAKE WITH LEMON ICING AND FOUR CANDLES, AND LEMON ICE CREAM.

Other Christmases

1969 - SINCE LAST YEAR MAN HAS WALKED ON THE MOON. A WEEK AFTER I TOOK MY FIRST STEPS, NEIL A. ARMSTRONG STEPPED OUT OF THE EAGLE IN THE SEA OF TRANQUILITY AND ANNOUNCED, "THAT'S ONE SMALL STEP FOR A MAN; ONE GIANT LEAP FOR MANKIND." (JUNE 20, 1969)

SANTA WAS EXTRA GOOD TO ME THIS YEAR. HE BROUGHT ME A TOY PIANO MADE LIKE A TYPEWRITER, A SET OF BLOCKS, A PONY THAT GOES WHEN I JUMP ON HIM, BUT BEST OF ALL, A DOLLY. I NAMED MY DOLLY "SUGAR" AS SOON AS I SAW HER AND I ALWAYS SLEEP WITH HER. LAST YEAR WE WERE IN OUR HOUSE IN GEORGIA, BUT THIS YEAR WE ARE IN OUR TRAILER IN BLACK MOUNTAIN.

1970 - WOW! I SAW SANTA LAND IN A HELICOPTER IN DURHAM, N.C., THEN WE WENT TO MIAMI. DADDY HAS BEEN WORKING, AND WE ARE BETTER OFF THAN WE HAVE BEEN IN A LONG TIME. SANTA WAS GOOD TO ME IN FLORIDA, BUT WHEN DADDY HAD HIS ACCIDENT IN MARCH, 71, MOST OF MY CHRISTMAS PRESENTS WERE LOST.

1971- SYLVA, N.C. I PULLED THE CHRISTMAS TREE OVER ON MYSELF. SANTA GOT ME A RED AND WHITE TRICYCLE. I SAW HIM IN A PARADE IN TOWN AND LATER AT THE UNIVERSITY I TOLD HIM WHAT I WANTED. I HAVE A BROTHER THIS YEAR, TOO, AND I BOUGHT HIM A PIGGY BANK.

My new baby brother!

This is the truck that my dad almost lost his life in. This accident changed the entire course of my life before I was even three years old. Most of us experience several of these unforeseen life altering events. The important thing to remember is these events may cause undesirable and difficult circumstances but they do not take away our ability to make choices and our choices are what determines our final destinations as well the circumstances that we will find ourselves in tomorrow.

Most of my childhood memories were of life surrounded by extended family members and filled with love in Gum Log, Georgia. It was a small community in the mountains of North Georgia on the border of North Carolina and only a few miles from Tennessee.

We spent summers in the many creeks, rivers and lake around the area. We camped on the banks and hiked through the woods. Every summer also included more than one backpacking trip with my dad which often extended up to three weeks.

Every summer also included a visit with my dad's family. We would gather at Nanny and Poppop's summer house with all of my aunts, uncles and cousins. Those visits were like a private summer camp. We did all the typical summer camp activities but it was with family that we only saw for those brief visits. The days were active and chaotic and the nights were giant slumber parties with lots of whispering.

As a child I didn't realize how poor we were, financially speaking, because life was always full. We were never hungry because my Granny always had a large garden that was worked and shared by the entire family. We would also gather wild fruit as a family. Berry picking with my aunts and cousins was almost as much fun as a day at the creek. The fresh desserts were so delicious I can still taste them and the hot biscuits and jelly in the winter made for some fine dining. The animals that my Granny and Paw raised on their small farm, provided eggs, meat and milk for the entire family.

For most of my childhood my dad worked as a baker at Young Harris College. It wasn't far from my elementary school so I would walk to the cafeteria after school and "help". While this activity would be forbidden in these times, nobody seemed to mind having a kid running around a very busy commercial kitchen. Everyone was extremely nice to me especially a lady named Granny Birch. In addition to cooking in the kitchen she baked wedding cakes there. I loved going on days when she had a cake order. I would just sit and watch her make beautiful roses that covered the cake and dream of one day being able to make cakes as beautiful as the ones she created.

I was always allowed and encouraged to cook as a child. I remember cooking by myself at three years old. When I was growing up, cooking wasn't considered a career. It was a job for uneducated people. My dad has a B.S. and was the only member of his family, or my mom's family, to have a college degree. No one could understand why he was working as a baker. Because it was considered as a low position, I was never encouraged to **become** a cook. My dad raised me to live life without fear of making mistakes and to be something great that no other woman had ever done. He had hopes that I was going to be a famous feminist. I was, in fact, supposed to be the first female fighter pilot in the U.S. Navy. Oh my, how dreams change! I believe with my whole heart, that without the fearless "you can do anything" attitude that my dad taught me, I would never have tried many of the things I do today, including making YouTube videos and writing this book.

When I was in high school my dad got a job with the U.S. Forest Service and we moved away from the mountains and my family. We moved to Greene County, Georgia which was about a six hour drive southeast of Gum Log. I visited often, but life definitely changed. Not just because of the move, but because my Granny went to Heaven about one year before we moved.

At this point it seemed like life moved as fast as it changed. I rushed through high school, where I was an excellent student and left a year early, to start attending college. Half way through the first year of college, which was my last year of high school, I met my husband. We were both working at Hardees in Fayetteville, Georgia while I was on Christmas break. He said he knew the minute he saw me that I was going to be his wife. It took him at least two weeks to convince me. So at 17 our life together began. Two years later we had our first child, and by the age of 24, we had our fourth child.

When I was expecting our fourth and final child, everything changed, because at 24 years of age, *I was saved!* I knew who God was my whole life because of my Granny, but I did not **know** God.

Shortly after I was saved, we moved to Claiborne County, Tennessee where our fourth child was born and where we have lived every since. We raised our kids, built our home and stumbled through life together.

These stories and observations are not intended to hurt anyone's feelings or solicit pity from anyone. They are intended to show that events that may appear catastrophic, are simply direction altering, unachieved aspirations are not necessarily failures and every bad decision is not always as it appears. There are only two kinds of people in the world, heroes and victims. Victims blame everyone in the world for their failure and misery. Heroes never give up because they have God. Our past should give us strength, not control us. When we finally give God control of our lives, He uses all of our experiences for His purpose.

Remember to put GOD first!

But seek ye first the kingdom of God, and his righteousness; and all these things shall be added unto you. - Matthew 6:33

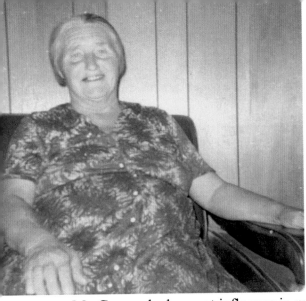

My Granny, Violet Adeline Stephens

My Granny had a great influence in my life. She is in a large part responsible for the person I became. She was that person in my life who had a true relationship with God, one that you could see. The way that she loved me and everyone else around her, taught me how to love. She also took the time to teach me how to cook, not just with ingredients or a recipe, but with my heart. She taught me that the food you prepare for your family is an expression of your love for them. She taught me that cooking is not just a chore, but it is a way of giving. My greatest sorrow in life was the day when my Granny went home to be with the Lord. I was only twelve years old and I did not believe I would ever be loved the way she loved me again. At that time I did not have a relationship with God so I truly felt I had lost her forever.

Twelve years later when I began my life as a Christian I understood what my Granny had tried to teach me as a child and I knew that special joy and eternal hope that she had. I knew that my salvation experience was real because for the first time in twelve years, that grief that I felt as a child was replaced with the faith that we would one day be reunited in God's house.

I truly believe that God puts someone special in the life of every single person He has created to show them His love. That person for me was my Granny. I also believe that every person who receives Jesus as their Savior has an individual experience and God gives each of us a confirmation that He is real in that moment. For me that confirmation was knowing that I would again see my Granny and the grief that I felt was relieved.

[14] But and if ye suffer for righteousness' sake, happy are ye: and be not afraid of their terror, neither be troubled;[15] But sanctify the Lord God in your hearts: and be ready always to give an answer to every man that asketh you a reason of the hope that is in you with meekness and fear: - 1 Peter 3

Pro God
Amendment 1
- Freedom of Religion, Speech, and the Press
Congress shall make no law respecting an establishment of
religion or prohibiting the free exercise thereof, or abridging the freedom
of speech or of the press, or the right of the people peaceably to assemble and
to petition the government for a redress of grievances.

Pro 2nd Amendment
Amendment 2
- The Right to Bear Arms
A well-regulated Militia being necessary to the security of a Free State, the right
of the people to keep and bear Arms shall not be infringed.

Pro America

I Pledge Allegiance to the Flag of the
United States of America,
and to the Republic for which it stands,
one Nation under God, indivisible,
with liberty and justice for all.

Menu and Meal Ideas:

Snacks/Appetizers:

Cheese Sticks
Chips & Cheese
Chips & Salsa
Onion Rings…57
Ham & Cheese Pinwheels…27
Cheese & Crackers
BBQ Little Smokies…52
Meatballs…44
Pigs in a Blanket
Cheese Balls…54
Fruit with Cream Cheese Dip…149
Veggies with Ranch Dip

Breakfast:

Breakfast Casserole
Biscuit or Toasted Sandwich with:
    Sausage
    Sausage & Egg
    Bacon & Eggs
    Jelly
Omelet
    Bacon
    Sausage
    Ham…46
French toast
Bacon …47
Eggs – scrambled or fried…48
Sausage
Toast
Biscuits…72,73,74
Pancakes…49
Waffles
Gravy…51
SOS…18
Hash Browns…58
Sausage Links
Chocolate Gravy…50
Muffins:
    Banana Nut…81
    Blueberry…82
    Pumpkin Spice…84

Lunch:
Sandwiches
- Bologna
  - With Cheese
- Peanut Butter & Jelly
- Peanut Butter & Banana
- Banana & Mayo
- Ham , Turkey or Chicken
  - With Cheese
- BLT- Bacon Lettuce & Tomato
- Grilled Cheese
- Fried Bologna
- Egg Salad…34
- Pulled Pork BBQ…28

Loaded Baked Potato
Sliders
Hot Dogs
Chili Dogs…23

Salads:
- Chef
- Caesar
- Garden

Blue Cheese & Bacon Wedge…62
Ranch Dressing…61
Chicken Salad…31
- Sandwich or With Pasta

Tuna Salad
- Sandwich or With Pasta

Soups:
Creamy Chicken Soup…32
Chicken Broth…29
Creamy Vegetable Soup…37
Chicken & Dumplings…33
Soup Beans…64
Beef Stew…22
Chili…20
Goulash…21
Potato Soup…36
Hamburger Soup

Dinner/Supper:

Any Breakfast Item
Any Lunch Item
Soup and Sandwitch
Hamburgers...24
Sloppy Joe...16
Cheese Steak Sandwich...26
Chili...20
Steak...17
Chopped Steak
Fried Taters & Beans...60, 64
Spaghetti
Lasagna
Pork Chops...42
Turkey...10
Hobo Meal...40
Fried Chicken...43
Baked Chicken...41
BBQ Chicken
Chicken Tenders with Onions
Chicken & Rice...45
Chicken Alfredo...38
Chicken Pot Pie...30
Salisbury Steak
Country Fried Steak...12
Stuffed Peppers...14
Meatloaf...19
Baked Ham
Pot Roast – Beef...8
Pork Roast...39
Hamburger Casserole...25
Chicken Casserole
Tuna Casserole
Shepherd's Pie
Salmon Patties...35
Sweet & Sour Chicken
Tacos

Sides:

Breads:

Desserts:
Pies & Cobblers

Cookies

Candy

Frostings

Toppings

Fillings

Dips

Drinks/Beverages:

Other:

Bret and I have a list of foods like this, just to make it easier to decide what to fix when I am too tired or busy to think about what to cook. I have left room for you to add menu ideas of your own. If it doesn't have a page number, look for the recipe in the next book.

Billy Graham was a great evangelist. I copied his Steps to Peace with God. I believe it is true to God's word.

Steps to Peace with God

1. God's Plan—Peace and Life God loves you and wants you to experience His peace and life. The BIBLE says: "*For God so loved the world that He gave His only begotten Son, that whoever believes in Him should not perish but have everlasting life*" (John 3:16).

2. Our Problem—Separation Being at peace with God is not automatic, because by nature you are separated from God.
The BIBLE says: "*For all have sinned and fall short of the glory of God*" (Romans 3:23).

3. God's Remedy—The Cross God's love bridges the gap of separation between God and you. When Jesus Christ died on the cross and rose from the grave, He paid the penalty for your sins. The BIBLE says: "*He personally carried the load of our sins in his own body when he died on the cross*" (1 Peter 2:24, TLB).

4. Our Response—Receive Christ You cross the bridge into God's family when you receive Christ by personal invitation.
The BIBLE says: "*But as many as received Him, to them He gave the right to become children of God, even to those who believe in His name*" (John 1:12).

* To receive Christ you need to do four things:

1. ADMIT your spiritual need. "I am a sinner."
2. REPENT and be willing to turn from your sin.
3. BELIEVE that Jesus Christ died for you on the cross.
4. RECEIVE, through prayer, Jesus Christ into your heart and life.

CHRIST says, "*Behold, I stand at the door and knock. If anyone hears My voice and opens the door, I will come in*" (Revelation 3:20).
The BIBLE says, "*Whoever calls upon the name of the Lord will be saved*" (Romans 10:13).

What to Pray (You can use your words. This is just what needs to be covered):

Dear Lord Jesus, I know that I am a sinner and need Your forgiveness. I believe that You died for my sins. I want to turn from my sins. I now invite You to come into my heart and life. I want to trust and follow You as Lord and Savior. In Jesus' name, Amen.

What just happened:

1. You are saved!
JESUS said, "*I am the door. If anyone enters by Me, he will be saved*" (John 10:9). The BIBLE says: "*Behold, I stand at the door and knock. If anyone hears My voice and opens the door, I will come in to him and dine with him, and he with Me*" (Revelation 3:20). The BIBLE says: "*Whoever calls upon the name of the Lord will be saved*" (Romans 10:13).

2. You are a child of God.
The BIBLE says: "*But as many as received Him, to them He gave the right to become children of God, to those who believe in His name*" (John 1:12).

3. You have everlasting life.
The BIBLE says: "*For God so loved the world that He gave His only begotten Son, that whoever believes in Him should not perish but have everlasting life*" (John 3:16).

What you do now:

Steps 1. Take a firm stand for Jesus Christ; make your life count. Tell someone about your decision.
Step 2. Get a Bible
Step 3. Read and study God's Word.
Step 4. Pray every day.
Step 5. Identify with a Bible-teaching church for worship, instruction, fellowship, and service.

Made in the USA
Monee, IL
27 January 2021